☆☆☆☆☆☆☆☆☆☆

The Story of
Our National Ballads

The Story of Our National Ballads

☆☆☆☆☆☆☆☆☆☆☆☆☆☆☆☆☆☆☆☆☆

BY C. A. BROWNE
Revised by Willard A. Heaps

"Give me the making of the songs of a nation, and I care not who makes its laws."
Andrew Fletcher of Saltoun (1703)

THOMAS Y. CROWELL COMPANY: *New York*

CONTENTS

☆☆☆☆☆☆☆☆☆

America's
National Songs

Sing, America, Sing

Too long your harp has idly hung
Upon the willow bough;
The land has need of valiant song
Not futile weeping now.

For while you grieve, remembering
A shining yesterday,
The morning of your youthful strength
Will quickly waste away.

Take up your harp, America,
And sing courageously,
Until your myriad throated song
Resounds from sea to sea.

Let woodland, plain, and haloed peak
In one vast harmony
Re-echo to untrammeled skies
Their song of unity.

Your future's golden years await
The day when laggard man
Has joined the mighty song of songs
The morning stars began.

Go forth invincible with song,
Loved land forever free.
With strength renewed like eagle's might
Achieve your destiny.

Then forward on your periled way!
The powers of darkness flee
Away, when your heroic hosts
Advance to victory.

Now sweep the strings with song again,
Let hills and valleys ring.
Lift up your hearts and voices, all
America and sing.

GAIL BROOK BURKET

CHAPTER 1

America's National Songs

A national song is one which has been accepted for a number of years by the majority of the people, and is sung, hummed, played, and whistled by them. Such songs may have been written to fit a special occasion or to celebrate an event in the almost forgotten past. A present-day singer may have no knowledge of the circumstances which prompted the composition, yet he can feel the emotion which the blending of words and music is intended to arouse.

A great song is timeless because it expresses a feeling common to all. Songs are "national" when they have become so much a part of the musical heritage of a people that successive generations accept and sing them without questioning their origin.

In writing of *Home, Sweet Home,* F. Lauriston Bullard has aptly defined national songs as those "which have the peculiar vitality that captures and holds the affections of the people, generation after generation, appeals always in the most simple and direct manner to some universal emotion of the human heart. The fashions or feelings do not change. New forms for their expression come and go, but the heart is never quite satisfied, save with the old songs, whose melodies and words are made dear and sacred by the countless associations which they have gathered in their pilgrimage through the years."

"They were sung by our fathers," he continues. "All round the world, under every variety of circumstances, they have proved their charm. They are haunted songs, haunted by ghosts of former singers. Other voices than ours join in the chorus. They won the people originally because, with genuine power, they gave fitting expression to some fundamental sentiment; and in every generation they have vindicated their worth by capturing the regard of singers and hearers who, only later, came to realize the retrospective associations which had made them precious."

The words of such songs need not necessarily be great poetry. They may or may not be elevating or inspiring. They must, however, express the desired sentiment or emotion simply. The poem must be direct and uncomplicated. A critic has even noted that songs acceptable to most people usually include a minimum of three-syllable words. The thought and meaning is the essential element.

The music is of prime importance. The tune must be easily singable; the range must be within the limitations of the average untrained voice. The meter or rhythm must be definite and uncomplicated. Though naturally fitted to the words, the tune should be able to stand by itself. Most

5

songs have choruses or refrains which are easily remembered and sung.

A national song may be patriotic or sentimental, but always it contains a basic appeal. The patriotic air sings of liberty and freedom, pride in country and flag and loyalty to them. Such a song expresses our desires, our hopes, our pride, and our love for our country.

The patriotic song may be exciting, or it may be serious. *Hail, Columbia* and *Columbia, the Gem of the Ocean* are intended to arouse intense feelings of patriotism, as is *The Star-Spangled Banner*. Of the latter, Nevada Senator Key Pittman said in an address at the centennial observance of its composition held in Fort McHenry: "When we hear *The Star-Spangled Banner* our hearts swell with love and pride, our minds quicken, our nerves tickle with exhilaration, our enthusiasm is unrestrained, and we are possessed of a patriotism that knows no fear of suffering or death."

The war song, a type of patriotic composition, possesses the specific purpose of either arousing loyalty to a cause or expressing pride of accomplishment. War is a test of national strength, and civilians need to be aroused to an appreciation of the ideals of freedom involved in the conflict. War songs can make a people relive past battles and victories and value the peace which follows. The soldiers need to be moved to ever-nobler daring and courage.

Though written for one or the other of the two sections of the divided United States, the Civil War songs expressed the same feelings an individual would have toward a country. The Union was one nation, the Confederate States of America another. But some of the enduring songs of the war period, like *The Battle-Cry of Freedom,* were sung on both sides, with slightly different words to fit the local situation. Others, like *The Battle Hymn of the Republic, Dixie,* and *John Brown's Body,* could be applied only to one section.

A great war song outlives the period for which it was written, and strikes a responsive chord in peacetime as well as in war, because it still expresses confidence and pride in our nation. Soldier songs, of course, seldom possess the dedication of spirit which is the basis of the true patriotic war song, and for that reason they often fail to endure except in the memories of the participants.

The patriotic song of sincerity and depth, with its prayer for divine protection of one's country, makes a profound appeal to the religious feelings of the individual in contrast to mere pride. *America, The Battle Hymn of the Republic, America the Beautiful,* and *God Bless America* all call upon a Supreme Being to sustain the nation. They explain the motto of the United States: In God We Trust.

A people, however, cannot always live in the white heat of patriotism. In times of peace the basic sentiments of the populace are love of home, family, and friends, and the security of the family group. This explains the popularity of *Home, Sweet Home, Old Folks at Home,* and many of the songs of Stephen Foster. Such feelings are universal, and the author-composer team that can touch the hearts of the people has produced a truly national song.

All songs accepted and sung by the people spring from a genuine and deep inspiration. This urge for expression is not any less when the composition is written on order, as

7

were *Hail, Columbia, Columbia, the Gem of the Ocean* and *Dixie*.

Of course, under the stress of great and moving events the writer is driven to produce a poem. In describing how he was compelled to write *Maryland, My Maryland* in the first days of the Civil War, James Ryder Randall admitted that he was possessed of "some wild spirit" and was in "a fever pitch of excitement." Julia Ward Howe composed *The Battle Hymn of the Republic* after she had been deeply moved by her first sight of Union soldiers moving into a skirmish. Francis Scott Key's composing of *The Star-Spangled Banner* during the British bombardment of Fort McHenry is the leading example of on-the-spot inspiration.

The urge to composition may spring from a less intense but none the less profound emotion. Samuel Smith's *America* and Katharine Lee Bates' *America the Beautiful* were the results of an overwhelming realization of the glory and grandeur of our country. Stephen Foster's simple melodies reflected a sincere feeling for the ordinary things of life.

A composer has the task of matching the words with appropriate music to fit them into a proper setting or mood. The music is often composed first, with the words added to fit the tune. Because a song is meant primarily to be sung or played, the music is often considered more important than the words.

The music of many of our national songs can stand alone without the verses. *Yankee Doodle, Dixie* and *John Brown's Body* are examples; their words are ordinary and undistinguished, but the tunes are irresistible. However, the successful combination of words and music is what makes a song powerful and contributes to its popularity and universal acceptance. Nor must the words and music necessarily be examples of the true art of the poet and composer, for, as one critic has written, "Any song of the people, whatever its emotions may be, has a right to be classed as national music even if it is not fitted to shine among the classics."

Each song discussed in the chapters following has been selected because for a special reason it has endured and found a place in the hearts of our countrymen. Regardless of the date and circumstances of their composition, these national songs have become the legacy of the American people.

☆☆☆☆☆☆☆☆☆

Yankee Doodle

Yankee Doodle

Father and I went down to camp,
  Along with Captain Gooding;
And there we see the men and boys
  As thick as hasty pudding.

Yankee Doodle keep it up,
  Yankee Doodle dandy,
Mind the music and the step,
  And with the girls be handy.

And there we see a thousand men,
  As rich as Squire David;
And what they wasted ev'ry day,
  I wish it could be saved.

And there was Captain Washington
  Upon a slapping stallion,
A-giving orders to his men;
  I guess there was a million.

And then the feathers on his hat,
  They looked so very fine, ah!
I wanted peskily to get
  To give to my Jemima.

And there I see a swamping gun,
  Large as a log of maple,
Upon a mighty little cart;
  A load for father's cattle.

And every time they fired it off,
  It took a horn of powder;
It made a noise like father's gun,
  Only a nation louder.

And there I see a little keg,
  Its head all made of leather,
They knocked upon't with little sticks,
  To call the folks together.

And Cap'n Davis had a gun,
  He kind o' clapt his hand on't
And stuck a crooked stabbing-iron
  Upon the little end on't.

The troopers, too, would gallop up
  And fire right in our faces;
It scared me almost half to death
  To see them run such races.

It scared me so I hooked it off,
  Nor stopped, as I remember,
Nor turned about till I got home,
  Locked up in mother's chamber.

DR. RICHARD SCHUCKBURGH

About 1775

CHAPTER 2

Yankee Doodle

Our sole song legacy from the Revolutionary War, *Yankee Doodle,* was, surprisingly enough, an import from Europe. The British brought it to our shores during the French and Indian War (1754–1763), and it was not until twenty years later that the colonial soldiers of the War of Independence adopted it as their own. Soon it became a definite feature of our struggle for freedom.

A British tune at the beginning, *Yankee Doodle* had become a purely American melody by the close of the Revolutionary War.

Few of our national songs have had as many differing accounts of their origin. It is difficult, if not impossible, to separate truth from legend, for each story appears to possess a basis of truth. One can only accept the most generally recognized versions and leave the scholars to argue over details.

The early history of the air is wrapped in mystery. Many

countries—France, Spain, Germany, the Netherlands, and Hungary—have laid claim to all or fragments of it.

The French claim that it was an ancient song of vine-yard workers. The Spaniards say it was a native sword dance originating in the Pyrenees region. The Germans insist that it was one of their harvest tunes. The Dutch tell us that it was a peasant song of the low country, to be accompanied by the noise of wooden shoes, with the words:

> Yanker didel, doodel down,
> Didel, doodel, lanther.
> Yanker, viver, voover, vown,
> Botermilk und tanther.

When the Hungarian patriot Kossuth visited America early in the 1850s, he claimed that the *Yankee Doodle* air was so similar to a native folk tune of his country that there could be no doubt as to its origin. But Kossuth was not right.

The tune seems to have been a part of the ancient heritage of most of the countries of Europe, and appears in the folklore of almost every nation. It would probably be close to the truth, however, to credit England as the source of the rollicking air.

During the period of the Commonwealth when the Puritan (or Roundhead) Oliver Cromwell rode on horseback into Oxford in 1653, he wore a hat decorated with a single feather fastened by an elaborate knot. He was following an Italian custom of sticking long feathers in the headgear of horses on festive occasions. This decoration was called a "macaroni." Implying that Cromwell was attempting to be fashionable in imitating the Neapolitans, his Cavalier enemies sang these words to *Fisher's Jig,* a catchy contemporary tune named for Kitty Fisher, a lady well-known in court circles during the reign of Charles II of England:

> Yankee Doodle came to town
> On a Kentish pony.
> He stuck a feather in his cap
> And called him macaroni.

This tune, *Fisher's Jig,* was the air to which the *Yankee Doodle* words were sung in the American colonies early in the French and Indian War. In June, 1755, the British general Lord Amherst was near Albany, New York, with an army made up of both regular (British) and colonial troops. The British soldiers and officers in their smart uniforms presented an impressive picture, in contrast with the raw American recruits, a motley group in frontier costumes usually far from new, often in tatters.

A contemporary letter writer commented thus on them: "Quaint and ludicrous was the appearance of these raw American volunteers as they came into camp; some in black suits, some in blue and some in gray. Some of them had long coats, some short, some no coats at all. Some had long hair, some short and some wore enormous wigs. Their march, their great variety of accoutrements and the whole arrangement of their troops furnished altogether a good deal of sport."

As the raggle-taggle band of reinforcements in their variegated, ill-fitting, and makeshift uniforms assembled at Fort Crailo, the old colonial mansion of the Van Rensselaer family overlooking the Hudson River, the British began making them the butt of jokes. The contrast was, in fact, truly laughable.

Dr. Richard Schuckburgh, a surgeon attached to the British staff, was a leader in these jibes. One day, while perched on a wall in the courtyard watching his tattered and unsoldierly-looking comrades, he concocted some nonsense verses which he adapted to the old English tune of *Fisher's Jig.* He recommended the song to the colonial officers as "one of the most celebrated airs of martial musick."

The doctor called his absurd song *The Yankee's Return From Camp,* and it is this version which survives as our *Yankee Doodle:*

> Father and I went down to camp,
>   Along with Captain Gooding;
> And there we see the men and boys
>   As thick as hasty pudding.

In its original form the song had ten verses. They tell of a Yankee greenhorn who had visited a military camp and on his return home tells of the things he had seen—the feathered hats, the huge artillery guns, the drums, and the bayonets. All the noise and commotion of camp life appeared to have thoroughly frightened him.

The doctor's joke, however, did not bring the result he

expected. The unsuspecting, guileless, awkward Continentals swallowed the whole jest, hook, line, and sinker. The song spread like wildfire, far beyond the scoffer's intention. Within a few days *Yankee Doodle* was heard over and over in the provincial camp. The nonsense verses were bad poetry, but the rollicking tune seemed to express the spirit of the young, undisciplined Americans gathered in the training camp. The tune sang itself. Every one could whistle it while he worked, sing it before the campfire, and march gaily to its quick, brisk rhythm. The fife and drum corps found it irresistible.

Yankee Doodle soon became an American rather than a British song. The colonials had turned the joke on their tormentors and were to use the ditty to good advantage two decades later during the Revolution. The author of the doggerel died in Schenectady in 1773 and therefore did not know of the uses to which his song was put.

The origin of the words "Yankee" and "doodle" is disputed. The most-accepted version of the derivation of "Yankee" is that it was taken from the Indian word "Yenghis" (which in their broad guttural accent sounded like "Yankies"), meaning the English, that is, the colonial Americans. The word, however, came to be used by the British to indicate every American, particularly a New Englander.

Etymologists more readily agree that a "doodle" was a silly, foolish fellow, a nincompoop. Therefore the word would mean an English (that is, American colonist) simpleton.

The first reference to *Yankee Doodle* in print was in a

1767 publication of Andrew Barton's comic opera *The Disappointment*. The opera, the first in America of which there is any record, included *Yankee Doodle* as one of its featured songs.

The earliest known mention in a newspaper was in the Boston *Journal of the Times* of September, 1768, which said: "The British fleet was brought to anchor near Castle William. . . . Those passing in boats observed great rejoicing and that the Yankee Doodle song was the capital piece of band music."

Yankee Doodle came into its own as an American national ballad less than ten years later during the Revolutionary War, in which it was used as the rallying song of the colonial troops. The Americans had few bands, for every man was needed for fighting. But the fifers and drummers were in every camp and every battle, and *Yankee Doodle* was their favorite selection.

Just before the war, Boston, with a population of sixteen thousand, was the leading American town. Its citizens were intensely patriotic, and the town was the center of strong resistance to taxation and the repressive measures of the British government. The British felt the situation called for careful watching. Beginning in 1768, when the Old State House was occupied by a Royalist regiment, the troops were encamped during seventeen long months in the midst of a population to whom they were thoroughly offensive.

While tension mounted, the soldiers drilled daily and marched through the streets. To the great annoyance of the "proper Bostonians," the English soldiers raced horses on the Common on Sunday and played *Yankee Doodle* just outside the church doors during services.

After the Boston Massacre in 1770 and the Tea Party late in 1773, relations between the Massachusetts colonists and the mother country grew progressively more strained. By 1775 a clash was inevitable, and the citizens began preparations for a final break.

The Provincial Congress meeting at Cambridge in February organized the militia, units of which were quickly formed. A regular program of drilling and practice in arms was begun. From the ranks of the militia Minute Men, so called because they had pledged themselves to assemble at a minute's notice in case of danger, were selected.

These soldiers were a band of brave, enthusiastic, and undisciplined country lads under officers who for the most part lacked any military experience. But when the war came, as it did at Lexington and Concord, they were prepared. What they lacked in arms and equipment they more than made up for in courage and resolution.

The patriots of the Boston region had been quietly collecting arms and ammunition and storing them at Concord. Toward the end of the winter of 1774–1775, the British commander at Boston, General Thomas Gage, had received orders to arrest the two most annoying and troublemaking citizens—Samuel Adams and John Hancock, the latter the head of the local committee of public safety—and send them promptly to England to be tried for treason.

Referring to the preparations of the colonists and the activities of Hancock, the British occupying Boston sang the following to their *Yankee Doodle* tune:

YANKEE DOODLE

Yankee Doodle came to town,
For to buy a firelock;
We will tar and feather him
And so we will John Hancock.

In April, 1775, Adams and Hancock decided to leave
Boston, and they sought refuge in the parsonage of the
Reverend Jonas Clarke at Lexington, sixteen miles from
the town. General Gage decided to combine the capture
of the two culprits with the destruction or seizure of the
military supplies at nearby Concord, to which the Provincial Congress had been shifted from Cambridge. Accordingly, on the night of the eighteenth he dispatched a
force of seven hundred troops from Boston by a round-
about route. At the same time Paul Revere was riding out
by way of Charlestown and William Dawes by way of
Roxbury to sound the alarm.

The clash on the next day, the nineteenth of April,
marked the beginning of the Revolutionary War. The
British more than met their match in the Minute Men
awaiting them at Lexington and were soon helpless against
the ill-clad militiamen filled with a fighting fury which His
Majesty's Forces had never before encountered.

When the full-scale battle had spread to Concord and
the British regulars had been repulsed and scattered in disorder at the North Bridge, their retreat was covered by
a relief column of troops under Lord Percy, hastily
marched out from Boston to the tune of *Yankee Doodle*
played on their fifes and drums.

But in view of their success, the revolutionists immediately appropriated the air. Throughout the remainder

of the hard-fought and long-drawn-out war, *Yankee Doodle* was openly accepted as their own, sung and played in all the major battles, including Bunker Hill. It was heard in both victory and defeat. When discouragement dogged the colonists, the tune revived their spirits. Successes were celebrated with its joyful strains.

British military custom provided that, when an enemy surrendered, the bands of the defeated captives would be compelled to play their own martial music as a token of their submission.

Accordingly, when the terms of the surrender of Charleston, South Carolina, to the British were being discussed in 1780, General Lincoln's forces were expressly forbidden to play anything except an American tune. *Yankee Doodle* was still claimed as the property of the victors, so while the British guard played *God Save the King,* the five thousand Americans, with colors cased, piled their arms, marching off as prisoners to the sound of their fifes playing *The Turk's March,* a brisk but thoroughly American tune.

Their vengeance came at the final surrender of General Cornwallis at Yorktown on October 19, 1781, when *Yankee Doodle* appropriately served as the postlude to the successful struggle for independence. In negotiating the terms of the capitulation and planning the formal ceremony, the American representative, remembering the humiliation at Charleston, directed that the sword of Cornwallis should be received by General Lincoln. Furthermore, he insisted that the British, on marching out to lay down their arms, should play either a British or a German air, the latter referring to the Hessian mercenaries so bitterly resented by the Americans. The playing of *Yankee Doodle* by them was specifically forbidden. Instead, General Lafayette directed that the American band should strike up *Yankee Doodle* in order to remind the conquered British that this was an American as well as a French victory.

And so, at two o'clock the British Army marched out from Yorktown to lay down their arms. Pleading illness as an excuse, General Cornwallis sent General O'Hara as his deputy, bearing his sword, to conduct the formalities. For a mile along the route, the brilliantly uniformed French were lined up on one side, the American troops on the other. Of the sixteen thousand Americans present, those in the front row were neatly but somberly uniformed, but the second row, according to General Steuben, an eyewitness, were "but a ragged set of fellows and very ill looking." Every British soldier had been fitted in a new uniform with a bright red coat, hence the contrast was vivid and sharp.

General O'Hara, on horseback, led the conquered troops in a slow and solemn step, with shouldered arms, colors cased, and fifes and drums beating a British march, appropriately called *The World Turned Upside Down*. At the head of the line stood the American commanding generals. Cornwallis' sword was presented to General Lincoln to rectify his humiliation at Charleston.

In a nearby field, a squadron of French hussars had formed a large circle. Into this area, their own fifes and drums silent and the Americans playing *Yankee Doodle* loudly, the British regiments marched and threw their arms into an ever-growing pile. Then, still taunted by the tune, they paraded back to their camp.

The story of how the song was given back to the British with interest was told in a poem, "The Origin of Yankee Doodle," by George P. Morris, the author of "Woodman, Spare That Tree" (John is John Bull, Jonathan the American colonials):

> A long war then they had, in which
>   John was at last defeated;
> And *Yankee Doodle* was the march
>   To which their troops retreated.

> Young Jonathan, to see them fly,
>   Could not restrain high laughter;
> "That tune," said he, "suits to a T,
>   I'll sing it ever after."

This is exactly what has been done. The song had become the unique property of the Americans, and from that time on it was a part of our national heritage.

England, however, did not give up the tune. It was published in a printed collection of music in Glasgow in 1782, and reprinted many times thereafter, as a British song.

During the War of 1812, there came a time when *Yankee Doodle,* by then accepted as a truly American song and recognized as such by the British, proved of value against the enemy.

As the war progressed, the British made occasional

thrusts against the New England coast, often attempting landings to obtain provisions and stores for their men-of-war. The harbor of Scituate, Massachusetts, a fishing village a score of miles southeast of Boston, was guarded by a new lighthouse located on its northern side. Its caretaker was Captain Simeon Bates, who lived there with his family. Years before, when he was sixteen, he had been a drummer boy during the Revolution, and his father served as a fifer in a Rhode Island regiment. The old drum and fife occupied honored places on the wall of the family's living room, and the two teen-age daughters, Abigail and Rebecca, had learned to play them.

After several alarms when British ships had been sighted off the blockaded coast, a company of Massachusetts militia was assigned to the town. A small garrison was set up in the lighthouse. But their discipline became lax when no enemy ships appeared.

On the morning of September 1, 1814, when the assigned guards were absent, the British frigate *La Hogue* appeared in the offshore fog. The ship anchored a mile from the lighthouse and began launching a boat with the apparent purpose of entering the harbor to seize two flour-laden ships tied up at the town wharf. Fifteen-year-old Abigail Bates and Rebecca, a year older, were alone at the time. They immediately realized that something should be done.

"Let's try to scare 'em off," said Becky.

"Let's!" Abby responded.

Rebecca seized the fife and Abigail buckled on the drum. Concealing themselves behind a shed near the lighthouse where they could not be seen from the water, Becky commenced playing *Yankee Doodle* on the fife while Abby beat the drum.

The boat was approaching the harbor entrance opposite the lighthouse when the strains of *Yankee Doodle* came floating over the water, as a call to arms. The boat stopped while the officer in charge considered the meaning of the music. He reasoned that a hot reception was undoubtedly awaiting on the shore. Watching aboard the frigate, the commander-in-chief became alarmed and fired a gun to recall the boat. The oarsmen returned to their ship and the *La Hogue* weighed anchor and sailed away.

There had been no guard or army to repel the attack, merely two quick-witted American girls using the martial tune to frighten the invaders away.

Yankee Doodle also figured in the signing of the Treaty of Ghent which terminated the War of 1812. After the document was signed, the burghers of Ghent planned an entertainment in celebration of the event, and wished to have the national airs of the treaty-making powers performed as a part of the program. The music director accordingly called upon the American representatives—Adams, Clay, Russell, Gallatin, and Bayard—to obtain the music of the national air of the United States. Opinion was divided between *Hail, Columbia* and *Yankee Doodle*. The former was well-known, but the Belgian director did not know the music for the latter.

"Perhaps one of you gentlemen can sing or whistle the air," he suggested. But none of the ministers was able to carry a tune.

"I have it," exclaimed Mr. Clay, ringing the bell to summon his Negro body servant. "John," he said, "whistle *Yankee Doodle* for this gentleman." The servant did so and the chief musician took down the notes. At the banquet on January 5, 1815, the Ghent burghers' band performed the rousing melody, with variations, in brilliant style.

The bands, fifers, and drummers of the Union Army played the air constantly throughout the Civil War. Many lampoons against both Federal and Confederate politicians and military figures were set to the tune during the war.

It has been used by opposing parties in many presidential elections. It is played by every band in the land today, never ceasing to quicken the pulses of its listeners.

Several poets have tried to fit better and more literary verses to the tune, but without success. America wants the old words and the old tune.

When Anton Rubinstein, the master pianist, gave the final concert of his farewell American tour in New York in 1873, after a long and successful career, he was so pleased by his reception and the fact that the box office yielded the largest receipts of any of the performances, that he wrote a set of thirty-nine variations on *Yankee Doodle* as a way of thanking this country. Five months later, in response to public demand, he scheduled a series of "final farewell" appearances. The program of the seventh and last concert was made up of his own compositions, the final selection being the *Yankee Doodle* variations, the last time he was heard in the United States.

The incomparable Paderewski later began to compose

a piano fantasy on the tune, but when he learned of Rubinstein's music and belatedly discovered that *Yankee Doodle* was not our official anthem, as he had thought, he did not finish the work.

Yankee Doodle is a truly national song. In the words of one of the later versions:

> Yankee Doodle is a tune
> That we all delight in;
> It suits for feasts, it suits for fun,
> And just as well for fightin'.

In contrast to stately and solemn songs, the tune is simple, free and easy, comical, and rollicksome. One commentator has said, "How gay and funny and brave it is, and how it enjoys itself! How it sets the mind dancing so that the feet are almost forced to dance, too! For *Yankee Doodle*, you must relax yourself, like a child at a circus." "There is nothing to excite our musical pride about this simple tune, for it is merely a merry little jig, which seems to be best when played by a fife and drum corps. Men laugh at it, yet they love it. They find all manner of fault with it, yet they still sing and whistle it," writes another.

Few Americans today would be able to recall more than scattered words of either the chorus or any of the verses of *Yankee Doodle*. The tune, however, is always readily remembered and whistled. Its brisk, rollicking and saucy gaiety and its associations with the history of our country will continue to assure for this song its own distinctive place among our national ballads.

☆☆☆☆☆☆☆☆☆

Hail, Columbia

Hail, Columbia

Hail, Columbia! happy land!
Hail, ye heroes! heaven-born band!
  Who fought and bled in Freedom's cause,
  Who fought and bled in Freedom's cause,
And when the storm of war was gone,
Enjoyed the peace your valor won.
  Let independence be our boast,
  Ever mindful what it cost;
  Ever grateful for the prize,
  Let its altar reach the skies.

CHORUS

    Firm, united, let us be,
    Rallying round our Liberty;
    As a band of brothers joined,
    Peace and safety we shall find.

Immortal patriots! rise once more:
Defend your rights, defend your shore:
  Let no rude foe, with impious hand,
  Let no rude foe, with impious hand,
Invade the shrine where sacred lies
Of toil and blood the well-earned prize.
  While offering peace sincere and just,

In Heaven we place a manly trust,
That truth and justice will prevail,
And every scheme of bondage fail.

Sound, sound the trump of Fame!
Let Washington's great name
    Ring through the world with loud applause,
    Ring through the world with loud applause;
Let every clime to Freedom dear,
Listen with a joyful ear.
    With equal skill, and godlike power,
    He governs in the fearful hour
    Of horrid war; or guides, with ease,
    The happier times of honest peace.

Behold the Chief who now commands,
Once more to serve his country, stands
    The rock on which the storm will beat;
    The rock on which the storm will beat.
But, armed in virtue firm and true,
His hopes are fix'd on Heaven and you.
    When hope was sinking in dismay,
    And gloom obscured Columbia's day,
    His steady mind, from changes free,
    Resolved on death or liberty.

JOSEPH HOPKINSON

1798

CHAPTER 3

Hail, Columbia

Though long deposed from equal rank, *Hail, Columbia* for several decades divided honors with the two other patriotic songs of the early days of our country, *Columbia, the Gem of the Ocean* and *The Star-Spangled Banner*. For many years it was played on every ship of the United States Navy when the colors were lowered at sunset, in the retreat ceremony.

A particular favorite in Europe, the song was often performed whenever homage was paid to America or to one of its distinguished citizens. This was the tune that saluted the first American warship to pass through Germany's great canal at Kiel. When Thomas Edison entered the Opera House in Paris on a visit to the Continent in 1889, the foyer echoed with its strains played by a resplendently uniformed brass band as the inventor mounted the grand staircase. Because it was a European favorite, many foreigners were for a long time under the impression that *Hail, Columbia* was our national anthem.

Unlike many other American patriotic songs, *Hail, Columbia* was definitely political in purpose and spirit. It sprang into being as a side issue in the dispute between Great Britain and France, arising from the French Revolution, and contributed to lessening an intense strife between the Federalists and the Republicans resulting from our reaction to the French Revolution. In the end it helped to prevent our government from interfering in foreign affairs.

It is difficult, if not impossible, for us today to realize that a song could have such a far-reaching influence, even though it was written in the midst of great public excitement and strain, and composed, as were most of our national ballads, to be sung from the stage or at some public gathering. To understand it at all one must understand the conditions that caused such intensity of feeling.

In 1789, while the newly founded United States was still in the first year of President Washington's administration, the French Revolution broke out. By the end of the second year it had reached its most frightful period. France had proved herself a valuable ally and friend during our War of Independence, and our country had hoped to maintain cordial relations with her, particularly since the basic ideals of freedom and democracy for which the strife-torn country was fighting were similar to those for which America had fought in throwing off the yoke of the British.

Our new country had almost unsurmountable problems of its own, and the President and his advisers sought valiantly to solve the many difficulties. The nation was deeply in debt and its paper currency was becoming worthless. The people were rebelling against heavy taxes brought about by the long war of the Revolution. Trouble with the Indians on the borders of the settled states was continuing. By 1797 our foreign relations, particularly with France and England, were strained to an alarming point, and the sympathies of American citizens were sharply divided.

The party which called itself Republican, led by Thomas Jefferson, Samuel Adams, James Madison, and Patrick Henry, was in sympathy with the French Revolution and the idea of extending aid as a nation to France. The Federalists, chief among whom were Washington, John Adams, Alexander Hamilton, and John Jay, deplored the excesses of the French Revolutionists and thought their example rather to be avoided than followed, leaning more to the side of England in the conflict which was raging so fiercely.

Washington's policies were moderate and statesmanlike, yet his actions were greeted with opposition so intense and bitter that today it seems unbelievable. He was the victim of a political spite which even went to the lengths of suggestions that he be guillotined! He was persistently caricatured and persecuted by the newspapers of the day. Abuse was heaped upon him. However, he advocated and secured passage of financial measures which put the young nation on its feet. He maintained domestic order and put a stop to the aggression of the Indians. The United States had barely begun to breathe freely after its own war, hence the President considered it wise for the country to avoid becoming involved in the disturbances in Europe.

Therefore Washington issued a proclamation of inviolable neutrality early in 1793. He was determined that it should be adhered to both in spirit and in letter. This it was that brought down the fiercest storm upon him. He was called a traitor by the opposition. The attacks upon him reached the height of their venom during the bloodiest hours of the French Revolution, when France went to war with England because King George III refused to recognize its Republic.

Having co-operated in Revolutionary times, the French expected our material aid, or lacking that, at least our moral support in their quarrel with our former enemy. The Directory was then in control of the government, and its actions and attitudes were so outrageous as to disgust even those Americans who were inclined to sympathize with France.

Indignant at our policy of strict neutrality, the French nation treated our representatives with intolerable insolence, even threatening invasion and the destruction of the ships of our rapidly developing naval and commercial fleet. It was at this time that our ambassador Charles Pinckney was said to have uttered the famous phrase "Millions for defense, but not one cent for tribute," though his words were actually more forcible—"not a damned penny for tribute."

Toward the close of Washington's presidency the arbitrary acts of France against this country seemed destined to force us into a conflict. This danger continued as John Adams began his first term as Chief Executive in 1797. The American minister to France was unceremoniously ousted, and raids began on our shipping. The President attempted conciliation, but our special ministers were treated with contempt.

By this time Washington had gone into retirement at

Mount Vernon, but again he was asked to take command of the Army and Navy, with the special rank of lieutenant-general, should war actually break out. A few excellent frigates—the *United States, Constellation* and *Constitution* (Old Ironsides)—had been completed in 1797, hence the country was not totally unprepared.

The ex-President, then sixty-six years of age and worn and tired from his long public service, finally accepted the commission on June 3, 1798, upon condition that he should not be called to the field unless an emergency arose which required his actual presence.

President Adams' government continued the policy of neutrality toward France. The people were still sharply divided into political parties. Some felt that policy and unwritten duty required the United States to support the cause of "Republican France," while other were for uniting with England. The most radical differences of opinion existed between the Republicans and Federalists.

All treaties with France were abrogated and army units were quickly formed and drilled. Congress, in session at Philadelphia throughout the spring of 1798, was anxiously debating what attitude was best to assume toward the combatants on the other side of the Atlantic. Very bitter partisan feelings had been aroused by the passage of the Alien and Sedition Laws of 1798, as an outcome of the trouble between France and England. Except just before the Civil War, party strife in the United States has never reached so high a point.

It was during this hectic spring of 1798 while the violent disagreement was at its height, that the words of *Hail, Columbia* were written by Joseph Hopkinson, a Philadelphia lawyer. He was the son of the great Francis Hopkinson, a distinguished patriot of Revolutionary times and one of the signers of the Declaration of Independence, who in addition to his accomplishments as statesman, judge, wit, artist, and author, was also a musician, generally considered as America's first native composer.

Joseph was born in Philadelphia in 1770 and was to die there in 1842. At the time of his birth, the city was the most centrally located of our large towns. For that reason the Continental Congress was held there. And though but five years old when the Revolution began, young Hopkinson must have witnessed many stirring scenes during his childhood. When he finished his schooling, he began the practice of law, and from 1828 until 1842 was a United States District Judge.

Fortunately, Hopkinson, in a letter to a friend shortly before his death, left a complete account of how he came to write *Hail, Columbia*. "Amidst all the political turmoil the theater was then open in our city," he wrote, "and a young actor belonging to it, Mr. Gilbert Fox, whose talent was high as a singer, was about to have a benefit performance the next Wednesday. I had known him when he was at school, so it was entirely natural that he should call upon me one Saturday afternoon in April. . . . He was in despair, saying that as twenty boxes still remained unsold it looked as though the proposed benefit would be a failure." His prospects were very disheartening, but he told his former schoolmate that "if only he could get a patriotic song adapted to *The President's March* he did not doubt of a full house."

"I told him," Hopkinson's account continues, "I would

try what I could do for him. He came the next afternoon and the song, such as it was, was ready for him. The object of the song was to get up an American spirit which should be independent of, and above the interests, passions and policy of both belligerents, and to look and feel exclusively for our honor and rights. No allusion was made either to France or to England, or to the quarrel between them, or to the question of which was at fault in their treatment of us."

Advertisements were inserted in the Philadelphia papers:

> Mr. Fox's Night, on Wednesday Evening, April 25. By Desire will be presented (for the second time in America) a Play, interspersed with Songs, in three acts, called *The Italian Monk*. After which an entire *New Song* (written by a Citizen of Philadelphia) to the tune of "The President's March" will be sung by Mr. Fox, accompanied by the Full Band and the following Grand Chorus:
>
> > Firm, united, let us be,
> > Rallying round our Liberty;
> > As a band of brothers joined,
> > Peace and safety we shall find.

The theater was packed. One cannot imagine the mere announcement of a new song attracting a capacity audience today, but it must be remembered that this theater stood almost within the shadow of the seat of government, and that the city was rocked by the passions of the people. This explains why the announcement of "a new patriotic song" could draw a crowd.

The song found favor at once; both French and English partisans took it to their hearts. It was encored and re-encored, in wild enthusiasm, more than half a dozen times. Before its seventh repetition, the audience, already familiar with the tune, had learned the words of the chorus, and finally rose and joined Fox in a thundering refrain.

Because of its success, it was thereafter included in all the regular performances of Fox's company, and the theater was again completely filled the next night. For many nights after that *Hail, Columbia* thrilled the eager audiences. President Adams and his cabinet, no doubt realizing what the song was doing to unite the people, attended in a body in order to hear the new patriotic air. Within a week it had been performed in New York, and before long it was sung everywhere and by all classes of citizens. Gilbert Fox reaped a golden harvest as its "one and only original performer," and attained a brief but enthusiastic fame.

Hopkinson sent a presentation copy of his poem to George Washington on May 9, 1798, writing in the accompanying letter, "As to the song, it was a hasty composition, and can pretend to very little extrinsic merit. Yet I believe its public reception has at least equaled any thing of the kind."

At first the song became known under the title *The*

Favorite New Federal Song, but it soon took as its title the first two words of the opening stanza.

The words clearly show true patriotism and devotion to country. The first verse expresses gratitude for Columbia's (America's) hard-fought independence. The second, without identifying the "rude foe," calls patriots to defend the country. The third is a paean of praise for and tribute to the accomplishments of Washington in both peace and war.

The fourth verse, beginning "Behold the Chief who now commands," has been the subject of some discussion. Some have thought that the stanza honored President Adams. But the words obviously refer to Washington, and form a logical continuation of the previous verse. The capitalization of "Chief" indicates his anticipated reappointment as Commander-in-Chief of the Army, a title which he had only temporarily dropped. The phrase "once more to serve his country" clinches the argument, for these words could not possibly have had application to Adams. These verses of *Hail, Columbia* therefore honored the contemplated recall of Washington at a time when "immortal patriots" were being urged to "rise once more" to "defend your shore."

The music that helped make the song a political success had been written several years previously. Although there is still much debate as to the identity of the composer, the melody was definitely written in 1789, the year of Washington's inauguration, and was titled *The President's March* in honor of the new President. It was apparently designed to replace *The Washington March* of Revolutionary days.

The musicologist Oscar Sonneck, after the most ex-
haustive research, finally came to the conclusion that it
was impossible to be certain about the composer of the
March, even though the music was popular and familiar
in its day. Because Washington was living in Philadelphia
at the time, either of two of the city's leading musicians
may have been the composer.

A son of one of the claimants asserts that it was played
for the first time as Washington rode over the Trenton
bridge on his way to his New York City inauguration in
the spring of 1789. This claimant was a German who lived
in Philadelphia from 1784 on, and died there in 1793.
His first name was Philip, his surname variously spelled
and reported by researchers as Fyles, Pfeil, Pfyles, Phile,
Philo, Phyles, or Phylo, with Phile appearing to be most
favored.

Some believe that the air was written by another German
musician of the city named Johannes Roth, who died in
1804. Others call him Philip Roth, due to the fact that
a music teacher of that name was listed in the Philadelphia
city directory from 1791 to 1799.

Though the name of the composer remains an unsolved
question, his music was destined to outlive the purpose
of its original composition, and to become one of the
country's truly stirring patriotic airs.

National songs are meant to be sung. The best and most
heart-stirring patriotic poems will soon be forgotten if not
supported by a melody which catches the public ear. It
may be said that Hopkinson's *Hail, Columbia* might have
conquered the nation with any of several popular tunes
of the times. But the fact remains that its immediate and

lasting success was ensured with the aid of the well-known *President's March*.

Hopkinson realized that his poem was written to fit a single occasion and was surprised at its continued popularity, saying that it had "endured infinitely beyond the expectation of the author, as it is beyond any merit it can boast of except that of being truly and exclusively patriotic in its sentiment and spirit."

The song was revived during the Civil War. When the Union flag seized from Fort Moultrie in Charleston Harbor was hoisted on the staff at Fort Sumter late in December, 1860, the band broke out with the national air of *Hail, Columbia* to the loud cheers of the officers, soldiers, and workmen. It was often played by Union Army bands during reviews and ceremonies in camp and on the march.

Hail, Columbia continues as a favorite, a vital point in its favor being that the melody comes within easy range of the average singer. Perhaps this is why it has always been beloved by the people, in spite of critics who have called it "the most threadbare of our patriotic outbursts," "of little musical value," "its poetry cluttered with bombastic and prosaic metaphors."

"At least," says Sonneck, "*Hail, Columbia* may claim the distinction in the history of our early national songs of being both in poetry and music a product of our soil."

☆☆☆☆☆☆☆☆☆☆

The Star-Spangled Banner

The Star-Spangled Banner

Oh, say, can you see, by the dawn's early light,
  What so proudly we hailed at the twilight's last
    gleaming,
Whose broad stripes and bright stars thro' the clouds
    of the fight,*
    O'er the ramparts we watched were so gallantly
      streaming?
And the rocket's red glare, the bombs bursting in air,
  Gave proof thro' the night that our flag was still
    there.
      Oh, say, does that star-spangled banner yet wave
      O'er the land of the free and the home of the
        brave?

On the shore dimly seen thro' the mists of the deep,
  Where the foe's haughty host in dread silence
    reposes,
What is that which the breeze, o'er the towering
    steep,
    As it fitfully blows, half conceals, half discloses?
Now it catches the gleam of the morning's first beam,
  In full glory reflected now shines on the stream:

---

* *"Perilous fight," in an earlier version by F. S. Key.*

'Tis the star-spangled banner: oh, long may it wave

O'er the land of the free and the home of the brave!

And where is that band who so vauntingly swore
  Mid the havoc of war and the battle's confusion
A home and a country should leave us no more?
  Their blood has washed out their foul footsteps' pollution.
No refuge could save the hireling and slave
  From the terror of flight or the gloom of the grave:
    And the star-spangled banner in triumph doth wave
    O'er the land of the free and the home of the brave.

Oh, thus be it ever when freemen shall stand
  Between their loved home and the war's desolation;
Blest with vict'ry and peace, may the Heav'n-rescued land
  Praise the power that hath made and preserved us a nation!
Then conquer we must, when our cause it is just,
  And this be our motto: "In God is our trust!"
    And the star-spangled banner in triumph shall wave
    O'er the land of the free and the home of the brave.

FRANCIS SCOTT KEY

1814

CHAPTER 4

The Star-Spangled Banner

Though long accepted as a national melody close to the American heart, *The Star-Spangled Banner* did not officially become our national anthem until March 3, 1931, when President Herbert Hoover signed Public Law 823, passed by the 71st Congress.

In spite of this recognition, no single patriotic song of the United States has been the subject of so much controversy regarding its merits as both poetry and music. Critics continue to contend that the words are not majestic and that the music is too difficult for a song intended to be sung on every patriotic occasion. The poem has been characterized as "fit only for the rubbish heap," "sheer doggerel," "the celebration of a very minor incident in our country's history," and "a sentimental song written in the midst of highly dramatic circumstances."

The music, while often praised as being both "dignified, harmonious, grand and inspiring," is characterized by some critics as "a degenerate barroom tune, a drinking song unworthy of our country's high ideals and standards of patriotism." The New York *Herald-Tribune* has editorially condemned the song as having "words that nobody can remember, to a tune that nobody can sing." Attempts to sing it have been termed as "an embarrassing struggle with both words and music." Yet no less an authority than the band king John Philip Sousa once stated, "What matter the words? The spirit is what counts. . . . It is a splendid march and no true American can fail to be stirred when it is played."

Regardless of the seemingly endless claims and counterclaims of its foes and supporters, our national anthem has been popularly accepted as a true expression of patriotism and loyalty to our country and flag. Certainly it is the outstanding song of the Stars and Stripes.

To evaluate this "flag song," we must know something of the evolution of our national emblem. In very early times there were many different kinds of flags in America, representing the nations which had settlements here and there in the New World wilderness. During the provincial period the English flag, with numerous variations, gradually came to be used from Maine to Georgia.

The first flag of the thirteen colonies, The Great Union, unfurled in 1776, had thirteen alternate red and white stripes with the red cross of St. George and the white cross of St. Andrew on the blue union.

The first truly American flag had its origin in legislation of the new United States Congress, on June 14, 1777. It called for thirteen stripes, alternate red and white, with a union of thirteen white stars in a circle on a blue field.

With the admission of Vermont and Kentucky, the stars numbered fifteen and were to be in three rows of five each, the fifteen stripes in alternate red (eight) and white (seven). This flag, used in the War of 1812 between England and the United States, was the one to which *The Star-Spangled Banner* referred.

When the British land troops invaded western Maryland in the summer of 1814, it was inevitable that their naval vessels would eventually enter Chesapeake Bay and attack the city of Baltimore, the harbor of which was guarded by Fort McHenry. The commanders therefore asked Mrs. Mary Young Pickersgill, a local seamstress, to make the largest flag ever flown in this country, so large that the British could see it on the fort's mast should they attempt to approach the city. The dimensions agreed upon were thirty-two by forty feet. When Mrs. Pickersgill and her twelve-year-old daughter began their work (for a fee of four hundred dollars) in August, 1814, they used a large space in a local brewery, working around the clock.

Raised over the fort when the attack celebrated in the song took place, it was damaged by eleven holes made by bombshells. After the unsuccessful bombardment and retreat of the British, the flag was presented to Lieutenant-Colonel George Armistead, Fort McHenry's commander. A large section had been cut from one corner to comply with a request of one of the defenders that his body be buried in a piece of the banner should he be killed, which he was. During the Civil War it was said to have been sent to England for safekeeping, but eventually found its way to the Smithsonian Institution where, repaired to a reduced size of twenty-nine by thirty-six feet and mounted on a firm canvas backing, it is now on exhibit.

To understand the fervor which caused Francis Scott Key to compose the poem of our national anthem, *The Star-Spangled Banner,* one must understand the situation in 1814, when our country was struggling through its second war with Great Britain. Fighting the finest army and navy on earth, the stalwart and outmatched Americans for almost three years had opposed the enemy, with alternate success and failure.

During the summer of 1814 the British had landed on the southern coast and, making havoc of villages and plantations as they advanced northward, had taken the city of Washington on August 24, burning the Capitol and the White House. The red glare in the midnight sky could be seen as far away as Baltimore. The English admiral George Cockburn notified Secretary of State James Monroe that the British fleet intended to demolish Fort McHenry by a concerted land and sea attack and then occupy Baltimore, three miles away.

At about this time Dr. William Beanes of Upper Marlborough, Maryland, led a party of local citizens in arresting and jailing some British Army stragglers who were creating a disturbance in a local tavern. Because he had "attacked a British soldier with a pistol," as the charge stated, he was arrested and taken aboard Admiral Cockburn's flagship of the British squadron. Only the fact that Dr. Beanes had been friendly with their officers and treated some of the wounded soldiers after the battle of Bladensburg prevented his being carried away, tried, and hung.

His friends were naturally troubled. One of them, Francis Scott Key, then a young lawyer practicing in Baltimore, determined to visit the British commander to seek the physician's release. Carrying a note from President Madison, Key, with a friend, John S. Skinner, went on the small cartel boat *Minden* under a flag of truce to the admiral's ship anchored in Chesapeake Bay.

He could hardly have arrived at a more inopportune moment, for the fleet was making rapid last-minute preparations for an attack on Baltimore and had transferred the prisoner, Dr. Beanes, to a smaller ship, the *Surprise*. While Admiral Cockburn treated Key with courtesy and agreed to release the doctor, he refused to allow them to go back to the city until Fort McHenry had been reduced, as he knew that the three Americans must have seen the preparations going on and would no doubt disclose the intended attack if permitted to return. Accordingly, Dr. Beanes joined his two friends on the cartel boat.

Key's frustration and disappointment at being compelled to remain with the enemy during the battle was heightened because he was a volunteer in the light artillery which was to reinforce the small force of regular army soldiers at the fort. These were commanded by his brother-in-law, Judge Joseph H. Nicholson, hence his anxiety was also personal.

The *Minden* was anchored near the mouth of the Patapsco River in full view of Fort McHenry. The three men therefore had a front-row seat at the subsequent bombardment, which began at seven in the morning of

September 13, and lasted intermittently for twenty-four hours.

Part of the British forces had been sent up Chesapeake Bay for a land attack on the fort from the north. This assault was to take place simultaneously with the bombardment from vessels stationed about two and a half miles away. Attacked from both land and water, the American gunners in the fort had a disadvantage from the start because the shells of their 42-pounders could not reach the fleet.

The suspense of the three friends on the little boat must have been almost unbearable. Key and all Baltimoreans had been told to watch the large new flag; its lowering would mean that the fort had fallen. As the sun set at the end of the day of periodic firing, the flag was still flying.

Sleep was out of the question, and Key peered through the night, though he could see the flag on its staff only when a bombshell exploded now and then and the fitful glare of battle lighted it for a moment.

After midnight there came a cessation in the firing, which was renewed an hour later at closer quarters. Key had no way of knowing that soon after midnight Admiral Cockburn had received word that the land attack on the fort had been successfully repulsed, and that unless it could be destroyed by the fleet the entire expedition would fail. This explained the fierce bombardment by sixteen ships at close quarters beginning at one o'clock and increasing in intensity throughout the early morning hours of the fourteenth. All that Key knew was that "the flag was still there."

Toward dawn the firing ceased. The moments that followed were the most trying and anxious of all, for, so long as the shelling continued, it was evident that Fort McHenry was holding out. Smoke and fog still hid the shore from the straining eyes of the three Americans.

The early morning hours found them still pacing the deck, impatiently waiting for the dawn that they might see the result of the bombing. Finally, "in the dawn's early light," they were rewarded for their long vigil. Through a rift in the mist Key's field glasses revealed the Stars and Stripes still floating over the American defenses. The attack had failed, in spite of the admiral's boast that he would carry the fort in a few hours and then the city must fall, a boast mentioned in the third verse of the poem.

The British had fired over fifteen hundred shells, each weighing as much as two hundred twenty pounds, without any effective result. They had been unable to approach close enough to level the fort because the channel had been blocked by the Americans with twenty-two vessels. Only four Americans had been killed and twenty-four wounded, mainly in the land attack. Fort McHenry had proved sturdy and impregnable.

Beginning with that thrilling moment of the gray dawn when he was first able to see the flag through the smoke and fog, Key had begun to jot down on the back of a letter which he happened to have in his pocket the opening stanza of the poem soon to become so celebrated. As soon as the British land soldiers had re-embarked, the naval squadron sailed away and the *Minden* was free to return to Baltimore. On the way back to the city Key completed the remaining three verses.

When he copied them later while resting in his room at the Fountain Inn, he found it necessary to make practically no changes. What he had written in the heat of emotion and relief needed little revision. Key took the verses to his brother-in-law, Judge Nicholson, who had just returned from the defense of the fort. He considered the poem so effective that the two went immediately to the printing office of Benjamin Edes.

Because the regular typesetters, members of the city's volunteer forces, were resting from their Fort McHenry duty, a fourteen-year-old apprentice, Samuel Sands, set the poem in type as a handbill or broadside, six and one-half by five and one-half inches, with the title *Defence of Fort M'Henry,* including a note that it was to be sung to the tune *Anacreon in Heaven,* which the judge had suggested as being admirably fitted to the poem.

The Baltimoreans accepted the song instantly. That very night Ferdinand Durang, an actor, mounted a chair in a tavern and sang *The Defence of Fort M'Henry* for the first time. The effect was an outburst of enthusiasm, for the tune was familiar to all as an English drinking song. Key rapidly issued five other broadsides, making in each a few minor but unimportant changes.

The first newspaper publication was in the *Baltimore Patriot* on September 20. By the end of the year, still under the original title, it made its first appearance in book form when it was included in *The National Songster,* published in Hagerstown, Maryland. The title by which the composition is now known was first applied early in 1815.

The melody *Anacreon in Heaven* is believed to have been composed in England between 1770 and 1775. It has been credited in turn to Dr. Samuel Arnold, composer to His Majesty's Chapel, and to a transcription from an old French air by John Stafford Smith. Anacreon was a Greek lyric poet whose works all glorified love and wine.

The name of the tune was taken from the words attributed to Ralph Tomlinson, president of London's Anacreontic Society, a social drinking and dining club, and sung by its members around 1778. The air was soon heard in the United States, where it was set to patriotic words. The most popular of these was *Adams and Liberty,* the verses composed by Thomas Treat Paine, an ancestor of the writer of *Home, Sweet Home.* Both Judge Nicholson and Francis Scott Key must have been thoroughly familiar with the tune, as were most of the Americans of the time.

Though Key's main claim to fame was the single poem of *The Star-Spangled Banner,* written when he was thirty-four years old, he became a distinguished lawyer and was later attorney-general of the District of Columbia. In fact, he was seldom thought of as a poet, though a volume of his verses was published fourteen years after his death on January 11, 1843.

In 1940 Francis Scott Key was nominated to the Hall of Fame, but received only eleven votes of the hundred electors; in the same year Stephen Collins Foster was admitted. Key lost again in 1945, and has not received that honor. But today a flag always flies over his grave in Frederick, Maryland.

The copy of the poem that Key wrote out in his hotel the afternoon of September 14, 1814, in the hands of the Nicholson family for almost a century, was finally acquired by the Maryland Historical Society for $24,000, and is now one of its most prized exhibits.

The locale of the song's subject has been preserved. Fort McHenry continued to be a military post until 1912, after which, in 1925, it became a national park, while its status changed to a national monument in 1939. In commemoration of the hundredth anniversary of the writing of the song, a buoy was anchored in Baltimore harbor at the approximate spot where the little boat with Key aboard was anchored during the bombardment—a buoy on which was painted a reproduction of the flag of which he wrote.

The Star-Spangled Banner has had a long and proud history. Between 1814 and 1864, fifty-four separate versions were published. During the Civil War countless new stanzas were composed to fit the times, including a poem by Oliver Wendell Holmes which was definitely anti-Southern. But none achieved any permanent acceptance. Throughout the years the song was our unofficial national anthem, but dissatisfaction with it on various grounds, mainly that the words described a single incident in the War of 1812, has led to several contests to find a new and more appropriate national song.

The showman **P. T.** Barnum instituted a prize contest for "the best national song" in the 1850s, but no awards were made. The contest was probably one of his publicity stunts. In 1861, during the early months of the Civil War, 1200 compositions were submitted in a competition for a national anthem, but none was considered by the judges of sufficient merit to be granted a prize. In 1928 a New York contest offering awards totaling $3,000 failed to produce a winning song, though 4500 entries were received. *The Star-Spangled Banner* still remains the nation's choice.

Unofficial acceptance came long before the 1931 legislation. In 1889 the Secretary of the Navy ordered that the song be played at both morning and evening flag-raising and lowering ceremonies on naval vessels. In 1903 it became official for "special occasions" in both the Army and the Navy, and officers and men were directed to stand at attention whenever and wherever the song was played.

In 1916, before the United States entered World War I, President Woodrow Wilson proclaimed *The Star-Spangled Banner* our national anthem, but this was not binding when his term in office was ended.

The road to official acceptance was a long and stormy one. Beginning in 1913 and continuing for almost two decades, both houses of Congress considered bills recognizing the song as the national anthem. During the 62nd through the 68th Congresses from 1913 through 1928, these bills were inevitably buried in committees, though some progress was made when hearings were conducted before the House Judiciary Committee in 1924.

In 1928 the Veterans of Foreign Wars launched a national campaign favoring the legislation, and enlisted the aid of more than eighty patriotic organizations in the country. In a school poll, many thousands of children voted two to one in favor of *The Star-Spangled Banner* as our national anthem. Before the end of the two-year campaign, five million signatures, including those of twenty-six governors, were obtained on petitions presented to Congress.

After extended hearings before the House Judiciary

Committee the bill was presented on the floor with sharp debate, passed by that body, and sent to the Senate in March, 1930.

Following a favorable report by the Library Committee and more discussion, the bill came to a vote only when the five senators leading the opposition agreed to a test of strength by remaining silent. Accordingly, on March 3, 1931, the last day of the 71st Congress, the Senate passed the bill unanimously, and the signature of the President finally made *The Star-Spangled Banner* the official national anthem of the United States.

The path to acceptance was not without violent differences of opinion on the song's merits and weaknesses. Hundreds of thousands of words have been written and spoken on the subject by friend and enemies. The "anti" element has been far from silent. Even though the law has been in effect for almost three decades, the differences of opinion about our national song are still very much alive.

Throughout the many years of its existence, the song has been sung and played in many different versions. Since a patriotic song is intended for large groups, its music must be easily sung. Musicians and singers have continuously objected to the wide vocal range and complicated rhythm of the tune. During two World Wars commissions of both the military services and the music-teaching profession attempted to establish standard and more singable versions. Many composers have arranged adaptations eliminating the usual vocal pitfalls.

So confused has been this deluge of variations that Representative Joel Broyhill of Virginia introduced into the 85th

Congress a bill to have a single "standard" version of *The Star-Spangled Banner* legally established, and even conducted hearings in the House Judiciary Committee in May, 1958. The bill was the result of a request from one of his constituents for a copy of the "official" version of our national anthem, at which time the congressman discovered that such did not exist and decided to do something about it.

In preparation for such action a committee of the National Music Council, a body composed of representatives from forty-six organizations, submitted a series of recommendations in the fall of 1957. These covered decisions of the exact wording where differences existed in various readings, such as singulars and plurals and punctuation, the melody, the rhythm, and the harmony. The result was to be completely singable and readable. But, like much Congressional legislation, the bill has never been brought to a vote.

Because of the continued argument about our national anthem, it is appropriate to summarize the pros and cons of the widespread discussion regarding both the words and the music.

It is possible to dismiss the objection that the words deal with a single event, for the lofty tone of the subject still expresses love for the American flag. The narrative, however, is complicated, the words stilted according to modern standards. A Gallup poll made during the second World War revealed that only half of those questioned knew any of the words, but, even more deplorable, 32 per cent of these Americans did not even know the name of their national anthem!

The supposedly true story of a soldier in the recent war illustrates the common lack of knowledge of the words of the poem. A sentry, on hearing a noise at night, was said to have shouted, "Halt! Who goes there?"

A voice replied, "An American."

"Advance," commanded the sentry, "and give the second verse of *The Star-Spangled Banner*."

"I don't know it," came the voice from the darkness, whereupon the sentry said, "Proceed, American."

Strenuous objections to the third verse were voiced during both of the twentieth century wars in which the United States has been allied with Great Britain. The stanza was anti-British at a time when unity was needed; phrases such as "their foul footsteps' polution" kept alive a schism long forgotten. This criticism has also been linked with contentions that the entire poem is too warlike for a peace-loving and friendly democracy. Supporters of this viewpoint often omit this verse entirely; in fact, few Americans have ever bothered to attempt to commit the stanza to memory. One critic has said that the entire poem is "contaminated with the odor of gunpowder."

Nor has the music been spared criticism. The much-publicized objection by prohibitionists that the tune is taken from a drinking song appears to be minor, since few Americans know the origin of the melody. Lucy Monroe, who attained fame by singing *The Star-Spangled Banner* over five thousand times during the second World War, agrees that the music is difficult for an untrained voice. Almost all singers are unable to handle the high notes in the middle section of the song, and usually merely hum that part or stop singing for a few measures. Most of the suggested simpler versions are in lower keys with the difficult passages rewritten. A singable version along these lines may eventually be adopted.

In spite of the hue and cry, *The Star-Spangled Banner* seems destined to remain our official national anthem. And no one can deny that it breathes the basic spirit of patriotism and love of the flag, in every line.

☆☆☆☆☆☆☆☆☆

Home, Sweet Home

Home, Sweet Home

'Mid pleasures and palaces though we may roam,
Be it ever so humble, there's no place like Home!
A charm from the sky seems to hallow us there,
Which, seek through the world, is ne'er met with
    elsewhere!

CHORUS
Home, home! sweet, sweet Home!
There's no place like Home!
There's no place like Home!

An exile from Home, splendour dazzles in vain!
Oh, give me my lowly thatch'd cottage again!
The birds singing gaily that came at my call—
Give me them!—and the peace of mind dearer than
    all!

JOHN HOWARD PAYNE

1822

CHAPTER 5

Home, Sweet Home

No song in the English language can match *Home, Sweet Home* in its expression of the common sentiment of love of home. Other national songs may appeal to patriotism, love of and pride in country, and loyalty to the flag. But this simple air uniquely touches the heart and therefore transcends any bound of nationality or language. *Home, Sweet Home* is universally acknowledged as the world's home song.

John Howard Payne, the author of the poem, came of old American stock and was a direct descendant of Robert Treat Paine, one of the signers of the Declaration of Independence. His ancestors settled in eastern Massachusetts in Pilgrim days, the name, with variant spelling, appearing on records as far back as 1622.

John, the sixth of nine children of William Payne and his second wife, was born in New York City on January 9, 1791, and was named after the doctor who attended at his birth. While he was still a baby, the family moved to Easthampton, on Long Island's eastern end. The Paynes lived there in a clapboard, vine-covered house which was the oldest in the village save one. Here he spent his childhood in the bosom of a closely knit and loving family.

This house was to be the only true home John Howard was ever to know, and was to gain world-wide celebrity as the subject of the famed song. Today a visitor to Easthampton can see it in an almost unchanged form, for in October, 1927, the town authorities appropriated $60,000 for its purchase to perpetuate the memory of the young boy who made it famous.

During these early years his father was principal of a local private school, but when John was ten years old the family moved back to New York City and then to Boston where his father earned an uncertain living as elocution teacher and private tutor. The teen-age lad discovered that he had a rare talent for acting. John became stage-struck. In those days a theatrical career was unthinkable for a member of a respectable family, and the boy's ambitions, his father thought, could be successfully thwarted by placing him as a clerk in a New York countinghouse when he was a bare thirteen years old.

But his working hours were endured only to permit him to attend the theater regularly and to practice his skill in writing, for which he had an inclination. During his mid-teens he formed a lasting friendship with Washington Irving, who was later to make John the character of the "poor devil author" in *Bracebridge Hall*. Fired with his love for the theater, Payne secretly commenced publication of a weekly magazine called the *Thespian Mirror*. So excellent were his drama reviews and articles that they attracted the attention of William Coleman, editor of the New York *Evening Post*. Assuming that the *Mirror* was the work of an experienced and mature critic, the latter proposed reprinting one of the articles. Knowing that his family would discover his undercover activities if this were done, the precocious lad visited Mr. Coleman in person to beg that his identity be kept secret.

The influential editor was so impressed by John's talents, handsome appearance, and social poise that he enlisted the aid of friends in raising funds to complete the boy's education. Hence it was that John attended Union College in Schenectady, New York, where he edited a weekly magazine and took a prominent part in college theatricals. But his education and stage training were abruptly terminated by the death of his mother and the bankruptcy of his father. Five younger brothers and sisters had to be supported, and it was this family crisis that gave John Howard Payne the opportunity of realizing his consuming ambition of becoming an actor.

At the age of seventeen, on February 24, 1809, he made his first appearance in public as Young Norval in the play, *Douglas,* at the Park Theatre in New York City. In the character of the young Scottish highlander, a critic hailed the boy's "extreme youth, handsome appearance and lithe, agile figure, together with the spontaneity of his acting." This was a period when child actors were popular, and Master Payne, as he was called, was hailed as a boy who "enacts more wonders than a grown man." "A more engaging youth could not be imagined," wrote one critic, "for

he won all hearts by the beauty of his person and captivating address, the premature richness of his mind and his
chaste and flowing utterances."

Young Payne toured the major cities on the Atlantic seaboard with the company. Everywhere he was acclaimed as
a genius. Paid large sums for those days, he became rich
and successful, clearing ten thousand dollars within a year,
a very large amount a hundred and fifty years ago. He was
thus able to pay his father's debts and make the family
financially secure again. That same year, when still seventeen, he played the role of Hamlet; he was the youngest
American actor to portray the character up to that time.
However, as the years passed, his popularity waned, for the
novelty of youth was no longer a magnet to draw audiences
to see him.

In January, 1813, he therefore sailed for England to seek
his fortune on the London stage. This was to be the beginning of his vagabond life in foreign countries. The War of
1812 had begun with Great Britain and, as an American
citizen, he was jailed on arrival in Liverpool and held for
two weeks before being released.

On his arrival in London, he obtained an engagement
at the famous Drury Lane Theatre through the sponsorship
of Benjamin West, the celebrated American painter who
as President of the Royal Academy had great influence.
Payne's London stage debut, again in the role of Norval,
met with acclaim equal to that he had received in the United
States. For five years, until 1818, he appeared in London
regularly, playing twenty-two characters, including Romeo,
Hamlet, and Petruchio. As a theatrical star he became a

close friend of such literary figures as Coleridge, Shelley, and Lamb. Washington Irving, the companion of his New York days, was then in London translating and adapting plays for the English stage, and their friendship continued. But as Payne grew older, his career on the London boards came to an end, and he began devoting his time to the writing and adapting of plays.

In this new vocation he was fully as successful as he had been as an actor. One of his tragedies, *Brutus,* produced and played by the famous Edmund Kean, a current stage idol, was unusually popular, enjoying a long run at Drury Lane. Money continued to pour in, permitting Payne to live extravagantly. But at the pinnacle of this new career he conceived the idea of becoming owner-manager of his own theater, Sadler's Wells. He proved lacking in business ability, and his brief experience in this area of theatrical endeavor landed him in debtor's prison.

In jail he translated and adapted a French drama in three days. It was produced within a fortnight, and the royalties he received permitted the author to satisfy his creditors and obtain his freedom. As a result of this success, the managers of Covent Garden sent him to Paris to view successful productions and adapt them as rapidly as possible for the English stage. Several were set to music by the composer Henry Rowley Bishop, the music director of Covent Garden, and presented as operettas, then termed music dramas.

Clari; or, The Maid of Milan was one of the collaborations of Payne and Bishop. In Paris it had been a ballet with music by the violinist Rudolph Kreutzer, to whom Beethoven had dedicated one of his most famous sonatas. But Payne turned it into a play with music by writing original dialogue and verses, interspersed with songs and choruses.

While he was working on it he was undoubtedly desperately lonely and homesick, for in a letter from Paris to his brother Thatcher dated December 31, 1822, he wrote, "My yearnings toward Home become stronger as the term of my exile lengthens. . . . I long to see all your faces and hear all your voices." This feeling he put into the words of the song which was to be the heroine's first and principal solo.

On the evening of May 8, 1823, the production was first presented at Covent Garden in London. By the end of the first act, which had featured *Home, Sweet Home* as a solo by Maria Tree in the role of Clari, John Howard Payne had become the talk of the town.

The plot was a mélange of sentimental foolishness. Clari, a young Swiss peasant girl, had been persuaded to go to a duke's castle on his promise to marry her. But the nobleman hesitated to wed a commoner and Clari, awaiting the decision which would save her from disgrace, was miserable and homesick. In this unhappy state " 'mid pleasures and palaces," she expressed her longing for her humble mountain abode in the aria *Home, Sweet Home*.

A reviewer in London's *Quarterly Musical Magazine and Review*, while terming "the plot hackneyed, the incidents threadbare and the sentiments undistinguished," wrote that Bishop was "eminently successful in one single air. . . . To *Home, Sweet Home* the most unqualified approbation must be given. It is simple, sweet and touching, beyond any air we almost ever heard. Never was any ballad so immediately and deservedly popular." Of the twenty-two musical numbers in the operetta, *Home, Sweet Home* alone was responsible for its success, and the tune was used in six variations throughout the five acts.

A London publisher purchased the copyright of *Clari* from Kemble, the manager of Covent Garden. Within a year 100,000 copies of the musical play had been sold, with a profit of two thousand guineas. Payne received nothing but fifty pounds from his libretto. His name was not even mentioned as the author of the words. Since he was on the salaried staff of the theater, Bishop was paid a mere twenty pounds for the music.

The composer had published *Melodies of Various Nations,* a collection of national airs, in 1821. The publishers wanted to print a companion volume the next year. Since he was able to locate only eleven tunes, they suggested that he choose other countries which had no known national songs, and prepare original compositions for them. Bishop, therefore, wrote an original tune to represent Sicily and titled it *A Sicilian Air.* As words he used a poem of Thomas Bayly, "To the home of my childhood in sorrow I came, and I fondly expected to find it the same." When Payne set words to this music in *Clari,* he used the same theme of homesickness.

Because of this deception, the music was extensively pirated, since it was assumed to be a folk air not protected by copyright.

The only other of Bishop's forty-four musical compositions which has survived is *Lo, Here the Gentle Lark,* a composition in the repertoire of every coloratura soprano even today. On the basis of the world-wide acceptance of *Home, Sweet Home,* the composer was knighted by Queen Victoria in 1842, the first musician to be so honored. But he died in poverty; on the very morning of his death on April 20, 1855, an advertisement appeared in the London *Times* proposing to open a subscription for his benefit.

The song attained unparalleled popularity in England, and the names of many singers were closely associated with it, either in the role of Clari or on the concert stage. Madame Anna Bishop, the wife of the composer of the music, was largely responsible for making the song known throughout the world during her long career. She had the rare gift of being able to sing the most difficult coloratura soprano arias and showpieces as well as very simple ballads. She sang *Home, Sweet Home* in China, India, Africa, and South America, often in the language of the country, for she was an excellent linguist. She even sang it in the Tartar tongue in Siberia, then a part of Czarist Russia.

Clari was first produced in the United States on November 12, 1823, at New York City's Park Theatre, where Payne had made his theatrical debut. There its London success was repeated. The critic of the *Mirror* wrote: "The music is the most tender and beautiful we have ever heard." The operetta, interest in which was largely due to the single song, was performed scores of times. But the chief fame in America of the ballad *Home, Sweet Home* was the result of its constant repetition by two singers with whose names the song became synonymous—Jenny Lind and Adelina Patti.

Jenny Lind, "the Swedish Nightingale," had created a sensation on her first tour of the United States under the sponsorship of the great P. T. Barnum. At the conclusion of her concerts, following an evening of astounding vocal display, the incomparable singer invariably brought tears to the eyes of her listeners with *Home, Sweet Home.*

At the conclusion of an American tour in December, 1850, she gave two concerts in Washington and was twice received by President Millard Fillmore at the White House. At the last concert, the President and his entire cabinet, along with Henry Clay and Daniel Webster, were in the audience. So was John Howard Payne, who had returned from many years in Europe and Africa, and was awaiting reappointment to his foreign service post in Tunis. After the diva had completed her scheduled program she turned to where Payne was sitting and sang *Home, Sweet Home* with deeply sincere feeling as a tribute to him.

The beloved song was even more closely associated with the one and only Adelina Patti, who made her American debut with sensational success in 1859 in New York City. Thereafter she alternated appearances in Europe and the United States, and it was during her tour of Northern cities in 1862 that she gave several concerts in the nation's capital. Since the President and Mrs. Lincoln were in mourning for their twelve-year-old son Willie who had recently died of typhoid fever, she was invited to the White House for a private appearance.

She sang a number of soprano showpieces, ending with *The Last Rose of Summer.* When she finished Madame Patti saw that Mrs. Lincoln was weeping and that the President was covering his eyes with his hands. Only then did the singer realize the extent of their grief and immediately regretted having selected such a sad song. Hoping to change their moods, she told her accompanist Strakosch to start a gay air. But in a choking voice the President asked her to sing *Home, Sweet Home.* The pianist did not know the air and up to that time Patti had never sung the song, though she knew the music and some of the words.

According to a contemporary account, the President "rose from his seat,went quickly to a small stand at the foot of the piano, took from it a small music book and placed it on the piano rack opened to the piece. Then he returned to his seat without a word."

As Patti finished, Lincoln thanked her with unconcealed emotion. Later Strakosch suggested that the song would be a perfect "positively final encore" to close her concerts and send the audiences home in a mellow mood. For forty years thereafter, Patti always sang *Home, Sweet Home,* accompanying herself on the piano, as a sign that her performance was finished. She is said to have sung it in public more than a thousand times, and was its unparalleled performer.

The success of the song marked the beginning of a decline in Payne's fortunes, and his life thereafter was full of disappointments. In an attempt to capitalize upon the popularity of the song, the team of Bishop and Payne produced a second operetta in 1829 with the song title as its title. But this failed to live up to their expectations. For the remainder of his life Payne became a wanderer, often a mere step ahead of his creditors.

While in Paris in 1831, he fell in love with Mary Harden, daughter of the American Minister to France, and followed her to the United States, where he worked for Mr. Harden on the staff of a commission to the Cherokee Indians. When that assignment was completed, he became the American consul at Tunis, remaining there for thirteen years before being relieved of his post in 1845. It was on his return to America that he heard Jenny Lind sing the song in his honor.

During the next few years he was the homeless wanderer pictured in the song. The original manuscript of *Home, Sweet Home* he gave to Miss Harden, and it was buried with her when she died. His reappointment to the Tunis post was long delayed, and he did not return there until 1851. He died on April 10, 1852, at the age of sixty-one, and was buried in the Protestant Cemetery of St. George's Church, where a memorial window was dedicated to him in 1881.

For some years after his death, Payne had been all but forgotten in his native land. In 1872, however, his dedicated biographer, Gabriel Harrison, read a paper on Payne before the Faust Club of Brooklyn, New York, and suggested that a memorial be sponsored by the club in the poet's memory, to take the form of a bronze bust to be placed in Prospect Park. As a result, two benefit performances of *Clari* were given at the local Academy of Music on February 4, 1873, the proceeds being augmented by an auction of the works of the club's artist members.

The statue was unveiled on September 27, 1873, in the presence of 25,000 people. At the ceremony *Home, Sweet Home* was sung by a thousand children from the Brooklyn public schools, a commemorative ode was recited, and a eulogistic oration declaimed.

This observance served to revive interest in both the song and its author. In 1882 the Washington philanthropist and art patron W. W. Corcoran, who had seen Payne on the stage in his youth, feeling that the body of the writer of one of this country's best-loved songs should have a final resting place in the nation's capital, began negotiations with the State Department for its exhumation and return to the United States.

At the Tunis disinterment ceremony no band could be found to perform the song, so an English captain played *Home, Sweet Home* on the chapel organ while the wife of the American consul of Malta sang its words as the body was brought into the chapel and placed under the recently installed memorial window.

On June 9, 1883, in the presence of President Chester Arthur and his cabinet, the body was entombed in Oak Hill Cemetery, Washington, D.C. The cortege, including a military escort, was over a mile long. The grave was marked by a white marble monument surmounted by a bust of Payne. Thus the wanderer finally lay at rest in his native land, though still many miles from the actual home he celebrated.

A memorial gate was dedicated to Payne's memory in 1911 at Union College in Schenectady, New York, where he had been a student more than a century before. During the ceremony Alma Gluck sang *Home, Sweet Home* and, as always in public performances, the familiar strains brought tears to many eyes.

The Boston Museum of Fine Arts in 1916 acquired a portrait by Charles Robert Leslie which pictures Payne as a young actor in velvet jacket and lace collar. This painting had been owned by Virginia Cox, a cousin of Payne and resident of Paris. At her death it had been purchased by an Englishman, Howard Payn, who had been named after the author by his father, a friend of John Howard Payne.

The original autographed score of *Clari* was purchased by an American collector in 1884, the time when the reinterment ceremony had revived interest in its author. In 1923 it was bought by Hiram W. Sibley, founder of the music library of the University of Rochester, where it is now in the collection of the Eastman School of Music.

The popularity and appeal of "the tenderest ballad ever sung," "pre-eminently the song dearest to the heart of the English-speaking race," is self-evident. There are several reasons for this universal acceptance.

Seldom have words and music been so well blended in a composition. The song has that unpredictable quality called "thrills" in the theatrical world. Its attraction does not depend solely upon the ability of the performer, for it speaks for itself.

More important, it expresses one of the deepest and most universal sentiments of mankind. In our hectic and busy world there is scarcely a man, woman, or child who has not felt the pain of homesickness, be that home a modern apartment, an up-to-date house, or a simple farmhouse of one's childhood memories.

No matter where, or under what conditions heard, *Home, Sweet Home* will touch the heart and mind of the listener and carry him back to the associations of his childhood home.

☆☆☆☆☆☆☆☆☆

America

America

My country! 'tis of thee,
  Sweet land of liberty,
    Of thee I sing.
Land where my fathers died!
  Land of the Pilgrims' pride!
From ev'ry mountain side,
  Let freedom ring!

My native country, thee,
  Land of the noble free,
    Thy name I love.
I love thy rocks and rills,
  Thy woods and templed hills;
My heart with rapture thrills,
  Like that above.

Let music swell the breeze,
  And ring from all the trees,
    Sweet freedom's song.
Let mortal tongues awake;
  Let all that breathe partake;
Let rocks their silence break,
  The sound prolong.

Our father's God, to Thee,
  Author of liberty,
    To Thee we sing.
Long may our land be bright
  With freedom's holy light;
Protect us by Thy might,
  Great God, our King!

SAMUEL F. SMITH

1832

CHAPTER 6

America

America has been characterized as the most devotional of our national songs. The tune is a worldwide one and is the music of the national anthems of two other countries, Great Britain and Austria.

Yet the majestic simplicity of the words linked quite perfectly with the most singable of simple tunes make it a prime example of an almost faultless union of words and music. Many have felt that, in spite of its being used as *God Save the King* (or Queen, depending on the contemporary reigning monarch of England), *America* should have been designated as our official anthem instead of its main rival, *The Star-Spangled Banner,* the words of which lack the depth of true feeling, and the music the simplicity required of a song to be accepted by the people and sung by them. *America*'s only rival of its type is *America the Beautiful* which, as a prayer, possesses even greater spiritual depth.

The truly American aspects of the words seem appropriately revealed by the author's name, Mr. Smith, the most common of English language surnames in America. When Samuel Francis Smith was born in Boston on October 21, 1808, the United States had passed the disturbing period of its birth pains (the time of *Yankee Doodle* and *Hail, Columbia*) and was entering upon an era of almost unparalleled development. The America to which Smith appealed in 1832 had a population of a mere thirteen million, concentrated mainly on the Atlantic seaboard. The West, to the Mississippi Valley and beyond, was yet to be explored and settled. Life was simple and the inventions which were to revolutionize it in every phase—customs and manners, arts and sciences, commerce and economics—were only beginning.

Young Smith enjoyed the advantages of a solid classical education, attending a private school, then graduating from Harvard College in 1829, when he was twenty-one years old. Choosing to enter the ministry, he studied at Andover Theological Seminary, and it was during his student days there that he wrote *America*.

His first pastorate after his ordination as a Baptist clergyman was in Waterville, Maine. His exceptional linguistic ability led to his appointment as professor of modern languages in Waterville (now known as Colby) College. For eight years he occupied these two positions. The college later conferred the degree of Doctor of Divinity upon him, and it was as Dr. Smith that his name came to be known throughout the world.

He moved to Newton, Massachusetts, in 1842, where he became pastor of the First Baptist Church. This town was to be his home for more than half a century thereafter. Church and missionary work occupied him for many years while he was editor of the *Christian Review* and secetary of the American Baptist Missionary Union. During the seventies and eighties he traveled widely inspecting missions of all denominations. During these trips he was able to develop his facility for languages, and eventually mastered fifteen different tongues. On his eighty-fifth birthday he began the study of Russian. Wherever he went, he heard his poem sung in English and many other tongues.

Dr. Smith's long and productive career continued through his old age. Once at a reunion of the Harvard class of 1829, Oliver Wendell Holmes mentioned each member in a poem entitled "The Boys." Of Smith he wrote:

> And there's a nice youngster of excellent pith,—
> Fate thought to conceal him by naming him Smith;
> But he shouted a song for the brave and the free,—
> Just read on his medal, "My Country, of Thee"!

Dr. Smith was active up to the very day of his death on November 16, 1895, at the advanced age of ninety-three, in a railroad station near Boston while en route to fill a preaching engagement. During his long life he had written nearly six hundred poems, the most famous of which, aside from *America,* was the hymn *The Morning Light Is Breaking.*

In the history of American music the name of Lowell Mason is in the front rank of pioneers. His contributions were many. Scores of his hymn tunes are still known and sung today, among them *Nearer My God to Thee, Blest*

Be the Tie that Binds, and *My Faith Looks Up to Thee.*
He compiled many books of hymns and songs. But above
all he originated public-school music in the United States.
It was while thinking, studying, talking, and discussing
plans for popular education in music that he made the
acquaintance of Samuel F. Smith, then a student at Andover Seminary.

In 1831, William C. Woodbridge, who, as editor of the
American Journal of Education, was interested in the new
developments and experiments in the European educational systems, returned from a trip abroad. His mission
had been to observe the German public schools with a view
of applying any new and untried features to our schools.
Finding that much attention was given to music there, he
brought back a number of their music books which contained words and tunes especially adapted for children.
These he gave to Mason for possible use in the new crusade.

Since the latter was unable to read German, he gave the
books to the young Andover student with the request, according to Smith's own account, "that I should translate
any of the hymns and songs which struck my fancy, or, neg-
lecting the German words, write hymns or songs of my own
adapted to the tunes so that he could use the music." The
result of Smith's first survey was the publication by Mason
in 1831 of *The Juvenile Lyre,* a slim volume of less than
a hundred pages, the first book of music for children to be
issued in the United States.

Smith's knowledge of foreign languages, particularly
German, led to the composition of *America* the next year.
In his spare time Smith went on with his analysis of the

remaining books. But let him continue the story in his own words: "On a dismal day in February, 1832, turning over the leaves of one of these music books, I fell in with the tune, which pleased me by its simple and natural movement and by its special fitness for childish voices and children's choirs, which was the object of my search. Observing at a glance that the German words were patriotic, I was instantly inspired to write a patriotic hymn of my own. Without attempting to imitate them, or even to read them throughout, I seized a scrap of waste paper and began to write. In half an hour, I think, the words stood upon it, substantially as they are sung today. I had no thought of writing a national hymn. I laid the song aside and nearly forgot I had made it."

Some weeks later he sent it to Mr. Mason, who immediately recognized its exceptional qualities. On the following Fourth of July he invited Smith to a celebration at the Park Street Church in Boston, and surprised the poet with the performance of *America* by several score children, one of whom was ten-year-old Edward Everett Hale. This was the occasion when the hymn was first sung in public.

Four years later a collection of songs titled *The Boston Academy* included the tune with Smith's verses bearing the name *America, National Hymn,* its first appearance in print.

Soon the song began to be sung in schools, at patriotic gatherings and at picnics from Maine to Texas. It found a place in hymnbooks of various denominations. Dr. Smith's words were translated into Latin, Italian, German, and Swedish.

The Civil War marked the beginning of its universal acceptance. It was sung at meetings held to encourage volunteering in the Union Army, to celebrate victories, to pray after defeats, and at military funerals. It was sung when the women on the home front met to pick lint and prepare bandages or to pack supplies to be sent to the front. The soldiers themselves sang it on the battlefield, in hospitals, in camp, and on the march.

In its original form *America* had only four verses, but from time to time Dr. Smith composed added stanzas for special occasions. For the George Washington Centennial celebration in 1889, for example, he produced this added verse called the Centenary Stanza:

> Our joyful hosts today,
>   Their grateful tribute pay,
>   Happy and free.
> After our toils and fears,
>   After our blood and tears,
>   Strong with our hundred years
>   O God, to Thee.

Because of his association with Lowell Mason, as well as the acceptance of his song by children everywhere, Dr. Smith firmly believed in public-school education for every child. For the celebration of American Education Week in 1933, the National Education Association unearthed two long-forgotten additional stanzas, probably written by Dr. Smith for a local school celebration, suggesting that they be sung to remind the pupils of the benefits of their schools:

Our glorious Land today,
　'Neath Education's sway,
　　Soars upward still.
Its halls of learning fair
　Whose bounties all may share,
Behold them everywhere,
　　On vale and hill!

Thy safeguard, Liberty,
　The school shall ever be—
　　Our nation's pride!
No tyrant hand shall smite
　While with encircling might,
All here are taught the Right,
　　With Truth allied.

These extra verses, however, do not add to the strength of the original poem and are therefore seldom included in modern copies of the song.

Dr. Smith freely admitted that he did not know that the music in the German song book was that of *God Save the King*, the British royal anthem, since it bore the title *Heil Dir im Siegerkranz*, which he also did not realize was the Prussian national song. "I wrote the hymn to suit the metre, which instantly appealed to me," he said. "I was not too versed in non-American music and was therefore completely taken by surprise later when I was accused of being pro-British because I had used the tune."

Probably no other single melody has been used with so many different words in so many languages and countries. The tune has created endless discussion, has masqueraded in more shapes, and has been put to more diverse uses, by more civilized nations, than any other single musical composition. Its history ranges through many hundreds of years, and reaches a peak of use in the eighteenth century. Today, because of its association with the English monarch and its acceptance as the music of *America,* it is probably sung or played at ceremonies and gatherings more than any other tune.

France has claimed the tune, based on the assumption that the composer Lully glorified King Louis XIV to its strains. Evidence has been produced that some French nuns of the convent of St. Cyr sang the air. Certainly it is true that French royalists often fitted words appropriate to the current ruler or pretender to the throne, with the phrase "Grand Dieu, sauvez le Roi" (God save the King), an exact translation from the English.

The Swiss have claimed that *God Save the King* was taken from their national hymn, written to celebrate the victory of the ancient republic of Geneva over the troops of the Duke of Savoy in 1602, and sung for the first time at an anniversary festival the next year.

But British claims, inextricably linked with those of Germany, seem to possess the only true basis in historical fact.

The first appearance of this tune in England seems to have been around 1607, when it was sung in honor of King James I, in an arrangement by the celebrated harpsichordist and court musician, Dr. John Bull, who was also organist to the monarch. The air appears in collections of music published in both 1611 and 1619.

The first English presentation of the music in its present

form, which Smith found in the German book, was in a Cornhill tavern in 1740, at a dinner party given to celebrate the capture of Portobello by British Admiral Vernon the previous November, and honored King George II. It was called *God Save Great George, Our King,* and was sung by Henry Carey, in his time a very popular composer and balladist. In acknowledging the hearty applause, he announced that both the words and music were of his own composition.

This was definitely established in 1795 when Carey's son George sought a pension from the British government on the ground that his father had written both the words and music of what had by that time been adopted as the royal anthem. The son offered solid evidence that his father had brought the song to Handel's secretary for help in arranging the bass. Handel appears to have previously been familiar with the tune upon which he had based a song dedicated to his patron, the Elector of Hanover, who became King George I of England on the death of Queen Anne.

Shortly after Carey's death in 1743, a suicide at the age of eighty, the complete song was first printed in a collection titled *Thesaurus Musicus.* His song, with its request to the Almighty to save the king from being driven from the throne, was to prove particularly fitting during the period of Hanoverian rule in England, when the Stuart Pretender, Charles Edward of Scotland, threatened the monarchy. It was first performed publicly in London theaters, Drury Lane and Covent Garden, in 1745.

Because the House of Hanover was of German origin, the song naturally traveled across the channel and was adapted to the rulers of many of the states of Germany—

Baden, Bavaria, Brunswick, Hanover, Hesse, Mecklenburg, Saxony, Schwerin, and Württemberg. In 1760 a Bavarian lutist arranged the work for that instrument.

For the next few decades the air seems to have been tossed back and forth, from country to country, much like a musical shuttlecock. In the Netherlands it appeared in a 1766 songbook of the Holland Free Masons. The first country to adopt it as a national song was apparently Denmark. In 1790 one Heinrich Harries published it with the title "A Song to be Sung by the Danish Subjects at the Fete of their King, to the Melody of the English Hymn." The tune became the Prussian anthem in 1795 when, with the introductory words *"Heil dir im Siegerkranz"* (Hail thee, in victor's wreath), it was sung before King Frederick William. This was the version which Smith came across many years later.

The anthem had already been introduced in Austria in 1782, and in 1796 the composer Haydn, who had spent much time in England, arranged it to words praising the Hapsburg King Francis I, who was also Emperor of Germany. Most of the German states had their own versions, all expressing devotion to the ruling prince. It was also used as a national hymn in Norway, Sweden, and Switzerland.

The British anthem certainly became the most widely accepted of them all. Composers—Beethoven, Brahms, Haydn, and Weber—have incorporated the tune into some of their major works. But the song is kept alive today through its acceptance by Englishmen and Americans.

Opposition to the use of the English royal anthem as an American hymn has been voiced from time to time. But as the bitterness and enmity of the American past are forgotten and as England continues to be a worthy ally and friend, the music of *God Save the King* and *America* has been accepted by both nations as an entirely fitting setting for the majesty of the respective verses.

Throughout his long life, honors were heaped upon Dr. Smith. During the Chicago World's Exposition in 1892, on the four-hundredth anniversary of Columbus' discovery of America, President Benjamin Harrison in a proclamation called upon the people to observe it "by public demonstrations and suitable exercises in their schools and other places of assembly."

In his proclamation the governor of Massachusetts recommended that at a given hour on the discovery date all the school children in the state should sing *America* together, in their classrooms and assembly halls, in one grand chorus. This honor was accorded to Dr. Smith in many other states as well. Its appropriateness was the more fitting in that the date was his eighty-fourth birthday. Special exercises were also held at the Chicago Exposition, which Katharine Lee Bates had visited earlier in the year on her western trip resulting in the composition of *America the Beautiful.*

On April 3, 1895, the city of Boston honored Smith with two testimonials in Music Hall. Ten thousand people, school children in the afternoon, adults in the evening, heard the beloved minister describe how he came to write *America,* and these audiences joined in stirring renditions of the song. Dr. Smith characterized this as one of the greatest thrills of his long life.

The author repeatedly made autographed copies of the

song in response to the requests of admirers, but the original version as written in 1832 on a scrap of waste paper five or six inches long and two and one-half inches wide, was given by his son to the library of his alma mater, Harvard University, in 1914. In accepting the gift, the librarian appropriately wrote, "This is one of the most precious bits of original manuscript which any American library could desire to own. . . . From both a sentimental and patriotic viewpoint, it certainly ranks among our nation's most honored documents."

America has several unique claims as a national song. It is a hymn rather than a patriotic air. It is peaceful rather than warlike. When composing it Smith crossed out the only verse with an allusion to war and military might, and omitted it in the finished song:

> No more shall tyrants here
>   With haughty steps appear,
>   And soldier bands.
> No more shall tyrants tread
>   Above the patriot dead,
> No more our blood be shed
>   By alien hands.

Another of the reasons for its popularity is its distinctively personal character. In the choice of the pronoun "my" at the very beginning of the poem, the author gave the song a meaning to the individual singer. And the air is easily sung and the song is appropriate for all occasions, for the young and old of both sexes.

Smith's lifelong friend, Oliver Wendell Holmes, once

asked, "What is Fame?" And in answer to his own question, he said, "It is to write a hymn which sixty millions of people sing—that is fame."

In referring to his classmate, he exclaimed, "Now, there's Smith. His name will be honored by every school child in the land when I have been forgotten for a hundred years. He wrote *My Country, 'tis of Thee*. If he had said 'our' the hymn would not have been immortal, but that 'my' was a master stroke. Everyone who sings the song at once feels a personal ownership in his native land. The hymn will last as long as the country."

☆☆☆☆☆☆☆☆☆

Columbia, the Gem
of the Ocean

Columbia, the Gem
of the Ocean

O Columbia, the gem of the ocean,
  The home of the brave and the free,
The shrine of each patriot's devotion,
  A world offers homage to thee.
Thy mandates make heroes assemble
  When Liberty's form stands in view;
Thy banners make tyranny tremble
  When borne by the red, white and blue.
    When borne by the red, white and blue,
    When borne by the red, white and blue,
    Thy banners make tyranny tremble
    When borne by the red, white and blue.

When war winged its wide desolation
  And threatened the land to deform,
The ark then of freedom's foundation,
  Columbia, rode safe thro' the storm:
With the garlands of vict'ry around her,
  When so proudly she bore her brave crew,
With her flag proudly floating before her,
  The boast of the red, white and blue.

94

The boast of the red, white and blue,
The boast of the red, white and blue,
With her flag proudly floating before her,
The boast of the red, white and blue.

The star-spangled banner bring hither,
    O'er Columbia's true sons let it wave;
May the wreaths they have won never wither,
    Nor its stars cease to shine on the brave:
May the service, united, ne'er sever,
    But hold to their colors so true;
The army and navy forever,
    Three cheers for the red, white and blue.
        Three cheers for the red, white and blue,
        Three cheers for the red, white and blue,
        The army and navy forever,
        Three cheers for the red, white and blue.
                                    THOMAS À BECKET
1843

CHAPTER 7

Columbia, the Gem
of the Ocean

"Three cheers for the red, white and blue" is one of the compositions most often played on patriotic occasions, particularly on the Fourth of July. Of all our national songs, *Columbia, the Gem of the Ocean* lends itself most happily to stirring performances by brass bands.

Honoring as it does both branches of the service in the third verse, this "flag song" has often been called "The Army and Navy Song," and is therefore particularly appropriate when both soldiers and sailors are participating in a martial celebration.

While it is popularly known as *The Red, White and Blue,* its correct name is *Columbia, the Gem of the Ocean,* and it was under that title that it was first sung in the Chestnut Street Theatre, Philadelphia, in October, 1843, its words and music credited to Thomas à Becket, an Englishman residing in the city.

By a singular coincidence, this second well-known song

96

of the flag was written in the same year in which Francis Scott Key, author of *The Star-Spangled Banner,* died. It belongs to what might be called the second generation of national ballads, along with *The Star-Spangled Banner* and *America.*

In England the melody is still known as *Britannia, the Pride of the Ocean,* and much printers' ink has been expended in attempting to show that the author of the American words based his composition on this British song praising its navy, and used music composed a few months previously. There may be some truth to this claim that America made unauthorized use of a foreign poem and tune. A comparison of the English and American verses serves to substantiate this claim, for the similarities could hardly be due to both authors being inspired with the almost identical words:

Britannia, the Pride of the Ocean,
   The home of the brave and the free,
The shrine of the sailor's devotion,
   No land can compare unto thee.
Thy mandates make heroes assemble
   With Victory's bright laurels in view;
Thy banners make tyranny tremble
   When borne by the red, white and blue.

When war spread its wide desolation
   And threaten'd our land to deform,
The ark then of Freedom's foundation,
   Britannia, rode safe through the storm.

97

With her garlands of vict'ry around her,
When so nobly she bore her brave crew,
With her flag proudly floating before her,
The boast of the red, white and blue.

It is well authenticated that in the early months of 1842, Stephen Joseph Meany, an English journalist who later became such a militant participant in the anti-British Irish (Fenian) movement that he was sentenced to fifteen years' imprisonment, wrote the words of *Britannia, the Pride of the Ocean,* the poem being given to a friend in London, who showed it to one Thomas E. Williams.

Strongly influenced by the *Marseillaise,* the latter composed the tune now associated with the words. At that time Britain's navy was supreme on the sea. The song, readily accepted by the sailors, quite naturally found its way to the United States, and undoubtedly became familiar to the Philadelphian who produced its American counterpart.

Additional evidence of its British origin has been given by former Rear Admiral George Preble in his historical work on the flag of the United States. In 1876, while preparing the discussion of *Columbia, The Gem of the Ocean* to be included in his book, he contacted Mr. à Becket, who attempted to establish his claim once and for all as its sole author and composer.

On the basis of the similarity of words, however, Admiral Preble favored the theory of its British birth. He points out that "red, white and blue" could not mean the American flag, inasmuch as the ranking order of the colors of our banner is blue, red, and white—the blue of the union with its stars included, then the alternate red and white stripes. On Great Britain's flag, this authority tells us, the proper order is red, white, and blue.

Admiral Preble also noted that the term "the gem of the ocean" was very odd and inappropriate when applied to our country, which is landlocked on north and south and which at the time of the composition of the song possessed a navy of limited strength. On the other hand, the term would quite accurately describe the island country of Great Britain, with its superior naval power, which was a source of great national pride. The historian therefore concluded that in 1843 Mr. à Becket, using "poetic license," altered Meany's words only slightly to suit American requirements, adding a third verse to honor Columbia's (America's) army and navy.

Whether of British or American origin, "red, white and blue" has remained the standard description of our flag, due mainly to its use in *Columbia, the Gem of the Ocean*.

The Englishman, Thomas à Becket, a talented musician and actor, had long been a resident of Philadelphia. In the late fall of 1843 he was employed at the Chestnut Street Theatre in that city. One day he received a call from David T. Shaw, an American fellow actor singing at the Chinese Theatre. The latter was planning his benefit performance in accordance with the custom of actors and singers of the period, and asked his friend to write a song for his use in that single concert.

According to à Becket's account, "He produced some patriotic lines, but I found them ungrammatical and so deficient in measure as to be totally unfit to be adapted to music. We adjourned to the house of a friend and there I wrote the first two verses in pencil, and composed the melody on the piano. On reaching home, I added a third verse, wrote the introductory and terminating portions, made a fair copy in ink and gave it to Mr. Shaw with the request that he should neither give away nor sell a copy of the work." While he was at the piano, he may have unconsciously adapted his words to the English tune.

The performance was an immediate success, and Shaw sang it nightly as a part of his regular act. For personal reasons, however, perhaps because he wished to be closely identified with the song he had made his own through constant renditions, Shaw did not see fit to respect his friend's wishes in regard to publication. A few weeks later, when à Becket was in New Orleans, he was unpleasantly surprised when he saw a printed copy of the song entitled "Columbia, the Gem of the Ocean, Written, Composed, and Sung by David T. Shaw, and Arranged by T. à Becket, Esq."

On his return to Philadelphia, the composer-author paid a visit to the publisher, George Willig, who said he had purchased the song in good faith from Shaw. "I produced the original copy in pencil," wrote à Becket many years later, "and claimed the copyright, which Mr. Willig admitted, at the same time making some severe comments upon Mr. Shaw's deception."

The author then made arrangements with T. Osborn of Philadelphia to publish the song in partnership. Within a week it appeared under its proper credit, that is, "Columbia, the Gem of the Ocean, Written and Composed by T. à Becket, and Sung by D. T. Shaw."

E. L. Davenport, an eminent actor of the time, sang the American song regularly in his performances in London. In this way it became extremely popular and was published there, again without any authority, by T. Williams of Cheapside (the composer of *Britannia, the Pride of the Ocean*) under the title *Britannia, the Gem of the Ocean*. He used some of à Becket's verses mixed with phrases from Meany's poem.

When à Becket visited London in 1847, still another unwelcome surprise awaited him, for he found the song claimed this time as an English composition by Meany and Williams. "Perhaps it is," he admitted wanly, "I being an Englishman by birth." The exact identification of authorship still remains unsolved. Mr. à Becket must have unconsciously stolen the English navy tune, though he continued stanchly to maintain that he was its sole author-composer.

Ill-luck seemed to have pursued the singer while he was in England. During this absence from the land of his adoption, his publisher, Osborn, failed in business, and the plates of the song were sold to Frederick Benteen of Baltimore. "And in this way," concluded à Becket sadly, "it went entirely out of my possession, much to my regret and loss."

Singularly enough, two of our national ballads, *Hail, Columbia* and *Columbia, the Gem of the Ocean* were written by residents of the City of Brotherly Love, on both occasions by obliging friends to help out an actor acquaintance who was about to give a benefit performance.

The strains of "Three cheers for the red, white and blue" are completely singable, the repeated chorus being readily adapted to stirring performance. Though *Columbia, the Gem of the Ocean* is not identified with any event of historical interest, it occupies a permanent place among the major lyrics of American patriotism.

☆☆☆☆☆☆☆☆☆

Old Folks at Home

Old Folks at Home

'Way down upon de Swanee Ribber
    Far, far away,
Dere's wha ma heart is turning ebber,
    Dere's wha de old folks stay.
All up and down de whole creation
    Sadly I roam,
Still longin' for de old plantation
    And for de old folks at home.

CHORUS

All de world am sad and dreary,
    Eb'rywhere I roam;
Oh! darkeys, how my heart grows weary,
    Far from de old folks at home.

All round de little farm I wander'd
    When I was young,
Den many happy days I squander'd
    Many de songs I sung.
When I was playing' wid my brudder,
    Happy was I,
Oh! take me to my kind old mudder,
    Dere let me live and die.

One little hut among de bushes,
  One dat I love,
Still sadly to my mem'ry rushes,
  No matter where I rove.
When will I see de bees a-humming
  All round de comb?
When will I hear de banjo tumming
  Down in my good old home?

STEPHEN COLLINS FOSTER

1851

CHAPTER 8

Old Folks at Home

Stephen Collins Foster is universally acknowledged as the greatest of American song writers. He was the first American composer to make the composition of music his sole profession. But, above all, he was the first American to express in his songs simple emotions that spring from the heart. His compositions are sincere and moving, possessing that rare quality of simplicity which has led John Tasker Howard to call him "America's Troubadour."

Foster's parents had settled in Allegheny, Pennsylvania, near Pittsburgh, in the early years of the nineteenth century. There Stephen was born, the fifth son and ninth child, on July 4, 1826, a day and date notable as the fiftieth anniversary of the Declaration of Independence; on this same day Thomas Jefferson and John Adams died.

To observe the patriotic event, William Foster had arranged for a celebration near his home, a large tract of land now within the Pittsburgh city limits. An elaborate open-air dinner had been planned and soldiers from the nearby arsenal invited. Just at noon, when the guns of the fort were booming and the band playing, Stephen was born, to the tune of *The Star-Spangled Banner.*

The boy showed a talent for music early in life. Even as a two-year-old, he would sit on the floor picking out tunes on his sister's guitar. At seven he learned to play the flageolet, a type of flute, and the next year the piano and banjo. School was always secondary to Stephen's interest in music. His family, devoted as they were, never understood or encouraged this interest, for, as pioneers, they considered the arts unimportant. They merely tolerated his ambition toward song-writing in the hope, fruitless as it proved to be, that he would eventually abandon his unconventional ways and settle down to a more respectable life.

The urge to compose came to Stephen while he was still in his teens. His first composition to be performed in public was a work for four flutes, called *The Tioga Waltz,* which he played with three fellow students of the Athens Academy at a local art exhibition on April 1, 1841, when he was fourteen years old.

Three years later his first song, *Open Thy Lattice, Love,* a serenade to a lady on a balcony, was published in Philadelphia, with his name erroneously printed as "L. C. Foster." After he had completed his schooling he organized and became conductor of a singing club made up of young men of his acquaintance. This glee club met twice a week at his father's home, and quite naturally Stephen began to compose songs for its use. The *Lou'siana Belle* was followed quickly by *Uncle Ned* and *Oh, Susanna!,* the first of his real successes.

The Cincinnati music firm of W. C. Peters published the first two without paying the composer. The first money Foster ever received from his music was for the last named, published in 1848 under the title *Susanna, Don't You Cry:*

> Oh, Susanna, do not cry for me;
> I come from Alabama
> Wif my banjo on my knee.

"Imagine my delight," he wrote, "in receiving one hundred dollars in cash! The two fifty-dollar bills I received for it had the effect of starting me on my present vocation of song-writer." Contrary to his expectations, the three songs were successful. *Susanna* was the first of his songs to be sung by minstrels and it became the theme song of the gold rush and the favorite of early pioneers in the West.

The firm was said to have cleared ten thousand dollars from their sale, a sum which was not shared with Foster, who was never a good businessman, and was often exploited by music publishers. Always in need of funds, he was usually content to receive a lump sum to meet current expenses.

Now launched in his profession, Stephen Foster plunged into a period of creative productivity during the 1850s. His marriage to Jane McDowell in 1850, when he was twenty-four, did not bring lasting happiness, largely due to the development of his drinking habits which were to lead to his death in 1864.

The list of his 189 songs includes at least ten which are still so familiar and beloved that, had he written no others, he would still be recognized as the first truly American composer.

Everyone knows and loves *Oh, Susanna!* (1848), *De Camptown Races* (1850), *Old Folks at Home* (1851), *Massa's in de Cold, Cold Ground* (1852), *Old Dog Tray* and *My Old Kentucky Home* (1853), *Jeanie with the Light Brown Hair* (1854), *Come Where My Love Lies Dreaming* (1855), *Old Black Joe* (1860), and *Beautiful Dreamer* (1864). So affecting and genuine are these simple melodies that it is difficult to choose from among them.

General opinion, however, places *Old Folks at Home* as Foster's most-loved composition. Though originally written in Negro dialect, " 'Way Down upon the Swanee River," the song's alternate title, is probably as appealing and widely known as Payne's *Home, Sweet Home.*

An interesting story is told of the opening line. One day in 1851 Foster visited the office of his brother Morrison in Pittsburgh.

"Morrison," he said, "I've got a new song, and I want the name of some Southern river with two syllables in it."

His brother suggested Yazoo, but he said, "No good, that's been used before." Then Morrison said, "Pedee," but again the reply came, "Oh, pshaw! I won't have *that!*"

Then Morrison took an atlas from the top of his desk, and opened to a map of the United States. Together they examined it until Morrison's finger stopped at the Suwanee, a little river in northern Florida.

"That's it! That's it!" cried Stephen delightedly. "Now listen." Hastily scribbling in the word on a piece of paper he held in his hands, he read to his brother the lines beginning " 'Way down upon de Swanee Ribber."

By this time several of Foster's songs had become a regular part of minstrel shows, particularly *Oh, Susanna!* and *De Camptown Races.* E. P. Christy's troupe was enjoying great success in New York, and he wrote to Stephen Foster asking for a new song, with the right to sing it before it was published. He also wanted to have at least one edition bear his own name as author and composer.

Because he did not wish to be known as the composer of Negro, or, as they were then called, "Ethiopian" songs, this was agreeable to Foster. The composer asked for five hundred dollars, but there is no record that Christy ever made such a payment. He probably paid only the usual fifteen dollars for the privilege of singing the song before its publication.

Old Folks at Home was issued by Firth, Pond and Company in October, 1851, as "an Ethiopian Melody as sung by Christy's Minstrels, written and composed by E. P. Christy." The company paid royalties to Foster, and 100,-000 copies of the first edition were sold. Changing his mind the next spring, Stephen Foster sought to be released from the agreement with Christy. However, printed copies, which poured from the presses in ever-increasing numbers, continued to carry Christy's name until 1879, when the first copyright expired. Future editions bore Foster's name, and the royalties on the renewed copyright editions, after his death, were assigned to his widow and daughter.

In 1935, *Old Folks at Home* was adopted as the official

song of the state of Florida, because it had made the name of a sluggish little stream in that state world-famous.

The fifties were the years of the rise and development of minstrelsy, and Stephen Foster soon realized that he possessed a rare gift for acceptable Negro tunes and that the spread of his songs would be more rapid if they were heard in minstrel shows immediately before or after publication. He decided, in his own words, to "pursue the Ethiopian business without fear or favor, to establish my name as the best Ethiopian writer."

Ministrel songs followed in rapid succession after *Old Folks at Home,* for Foster had found his true calling. He wrote the words for nearly all of his songs, and being of an affectionate, tender-hearted disposition, many reflect his personal feelings.

His Negro songs were never inspired by spirituals. His identification with the slave came about only by his association with minstrelsy and the resultant use of subjects related to the supposedly happy and carefree life in the ante-bellum Southern states.

He was apparently attracted by the atmosphere of those plantations where the Negroes were well treated. A writer has observed, "The humming bees, the strumming banjos, cotton fields and the bench by the old cabin door had a warm and genuine appeal to him. He saw romance and beauty in the old South, the rustic way of life on the old plantations." Because he was not an Abolitionist, he may possibly have wished to offset the unpleasant picture of slave life given in Harriet Beecher Stowe's 1851 novel, *Uncle Tom's Cabin.*

Massa's in de Cold, Cold Ground expressed the loneliness and sorrow of a slave who had lost his beloved master:

> Down in de cornfield
> Hear dat mournful sound:
> All de darkeys am aweeping,
> Massa's in de cold, cold ground.

Though the song was used by Christy, Foster's name always appears on the title page of printed copies.

A beautiful setter he had owned was the inspiration for *Old Dog Tray:*

> Old dog Tray's ever faithful,
> Grief cannot drive him away.
> He's gentle, he is kind;
> I'll never, never find
> A better friend than old dog Tray.

To many *My Old Kentucky Home* is the equal of *Old Folks at Home* in sentiment. Foster and his sister frequently visited their second cousin, Judge John Rowan, at his home, Federal Hill, in Bardstown, Kentucky. The song was said to have been written one morning while they were in the yard, listening to the mockingbirds and watching the pickaninnies at play:

> The sun shines bright in the old Kentucky home,
> 'Tis summer, the darkies are gay,
> The corntop's ripe and the meadow's in the bloom,
> While the birds make music all the day. . . .

CHORUS

Weep no more, my lady, oh, weep no more today!
We will sing one song for the old Kentucky home,
For the old Kentucky home, far away.

Within a year after its publication *My Old Kentucky Home* had sold 90,000 copies on which Foster received a 10 per cent royalty, the beginning of a new publishing arrangement with Firth of New York.

In 1922 proud Kentuckians purchased the mansion for $65,000 and deeded it to the state as a shrine.

After the publication of *My Old Kentucky Home* in 1853, Foster decided to settle in New York City, where he remained over a year. He wrote *Jeanie with the Light Brown Hair,* and though one of his most popular songs today, it was less successful at first than some of the others. The Jeanie of the title is supposedly Jane, his wife, from whom he had been separated, though they were reconciled at about the time of its publication:

I dream of Jeanie with the light brown hair,
Borne, like a vapor, on the summer air. . . .
Many were the wild notes her merry voice would pour,
Many were the blithe birds that warbled them o'er.

This type of sentiment, popular at the time, characterized scores of Stephen Foster's love ballads.

When radio was in its prime in 1941, the networks rebelled at paying fees for the performance of music copyrighted by members of ASCAP (American Society of Composers, Authors and Publishers). As a result, the air was filled for the main part with tunes in the public domain, that is, songs on which the copyright period of fifty-six years had expired. *Jeanie with the Light Brown Hair* was resurrected, and became the most-played song on the radio for several months.

Homesickness caused Foster to leave New York City, and he returned to Pittsburgh, where he remained until 1860. This period marked the renewal of his domestic troubles, and he began to be plagued by financial difficulties. His songs were still enjoying enormous sales. By the latter part of 1854 his publishers announced the following sales figures: *Old Folks at Home,* 130,000 copies; *My Old Kentucky Home,* 90,000; *Massa's in de Cold, Cold Ground,* 74,000; and *Old Dog Tray,* 48,000.

Come Where My Love Lies Dreaming was his main new song during this time:

> Come where my love lies dreaming,
> Dreaming the happy hours away,
> In visions bright redeeming
> The fleeting joys of day.

In view of his excellent publishing contracts, it is hard to understand why Foster was so plagued with money difficulties during this period. He was constantly forced to draw royalty funds in advance, and his compositions began to lack the inspiration and fire of his previous songs.

In the fall of 1860, another separation from his wife having taken place, Foster returned to New York City.

Old Black Joe was published at that time. The Joe of the title had been a servant in the home of Jane McDowell, and Stephen had always been met at the door by him when courting her in the days when he was a struggling young song writer. "Some day I am going to put you in a song," Foster had said.

Though the old Negro was dead before the promise was carried out, *Old Black Joe* perpetuated his memory:

Gone are the days when my heart was young and gay,
Gone are the friends from the cotton fields away,
Gone from the earth to a better land I know,
I hear their gentle voices calling, "Old Black Joe."

CHORUS
I'm coming, I'm coming, for my head is bending low:
I hear those gentle voices calling, "Old Black Joe."

The song marked a turning point in Foster's work, for this was one of the first of his Negro airs not in dialect. The days of his minstrel songs were now in the past. Students of the composer also note the feeling of sadness in his works at this time, a possible reflection of his memories when his own life was happier.

With the coming of the Civil War, Stephen Foster began writing a series of topical war songs, nineteen in number, in addition to his usual heart songs and ballads, and twenty sacred compositions included in hymnals for churches and Sunday schools. Many of these wartime compositions were obviously turned out rapidly as hack work to obtain immediate funds to satisfy his increasing use of alcohol. None of them compares in the least with his other works.

However, during this three-year period, he composed one of his best-loved songs, *Beautiful Dreamer,* in 1862, though it was not published until after his death:

> Beautiful dreamer, queen of my song,
> List while I woo thee with soft melody;
> Gone are the cares of life's busy throng—
> Beautiful dreamer, awake unto me.

A story is told that in June, 1863, Foster and Dan Emmett were talking over war topics when they saw through the window a brigade passing on its way to the front, led by a band playing *I Wish I Was in Dixie.*

"That's your song," said Foster to his friend.

Presently another regiment marched by. Its band was playing *Old Folks at Home.*

"That's yours," rejoined Emmett.

The tale of Stephen Foster's decline and death is a pathetic one, and has been compared to that of Edgar Allan Poe. Suffice it to say that, according to a contemporary writer, "at times he walked the streets in an old glazed cap and shabby clothing, which made him look more like a tramp than the composer of songs that were being sung on every side."

Due to fever brought on either by his weakened physical condition or by alcoholism, he slipped one day and in falling struck his head against a stove, fracturing his skull. After three days of unconsciousness in Bellevue Hospital, where his identity was not known, he died on January

8, 1864, at the age of thirty-eight. His body was claimed at the morgue by his wife and returned to Pittsburgh for burial. At the graveside in Allegheny Cemetery, a band composed of local musicians played two of his songs, *Come Where My Love Lies Dreaming* and *Old Folks at Home*.

Critics agree that the power of Foster's compositions lies in their simplicity. They are easily played and sung, and are based upon three of the simplest chords in music. His influence upon the musical life of America is everywhere acknowledged. The depth of his sincere feeling raised the contemporary standards of taste, and his Negro melodies have attained the position of true folk music. The songs of few balladeers have lived as long, and have gained such a secure place in the hearts of a people. *Old Folks at Home* has been called "the most supreme contribution that has been made to what might be called the true folk song of white America."

Honors have been heaped upon this gentle soul. In 1937, a Foster Memorial was dedicated at the University of Pittsburgh, and thousands of manuscripts, letters, pictures, books, and mementos have been assembled there in a small building near the skyscraper Cathedral of Learning.

In 1940 Stephen Collins Foster was elected to the Hall of Fame at New York University, the first musician to be so honored. The memorial bust stands in the colonnade between Daniel Boone and James Whistler. Carved underneath are two bars of *Old Folks at Home* and the words

Way down upon de Swanee Ribber
Far, far away.

A white marble bust of the composer was unveiled in the main lobby of the Library of Congress, our national library, in 1953. According to the inscription it was "The Gift of Fellow Americans." Few composers belong to the true American tradition. Stephen Foster retains his place as leader of that group, after nearly a hundred years.

☆☆☆☆☆☆☆☆☆☆

Dixie

Dixie

I wish I was in de land ob cotton,
Old times dar am not forgotten,
   Look away! Look away! Look away! Dixie Land.
In Dixie Land whar' I was born in,
Early on one frosty mornin',
   Look away! etc.

CHORUS

Den I wish I was in Dixie, Hoo-ray! Hoo-ray!
In Dixie Land, I'll take my stand to lib and die in
    Dixie;
Away, away, away down south in Dixie,
Away, away, away down south in Dixie.

Old Missus marry Will-de-weaber,
Willium was a gay deceaber;
   Look away! etc.
But when he put his arms around 'er
He smiled as fierce as a forty-pounder,
   Look away! etc.

His face was sharp as a butcher's cleaber,
But dat did not seem to greab 'er;
   Look away! etc.

Old Missus acted the foolish part,
And died for a man dat broke her heart,
   Look away! etc.

Now here's a health to the next old Missus,
And all de gals dat want to kiss us;
   Look away! etc.
But if you want to drive 'way sorrow,
Come and hear dis song to-morrow,
   Look away! etc.

Dar's buckwheat cakes an' Injun batter,
Makes you fat or a little fatter;
   Look away! etc.
Den hoe it down and scratch your grabble,
To Dixie's land I'm bound to trabble,
   Look away! etc.

DANIEL DECATUR EMMETT

1859

CHAPTER 9

Dixie

Both *Dixie* and its Northern counterpart, *John Brown's Body,* were sung by soldiers during all the years of the Civil War, and exerted a mighty influence upon hearers as well as performers. Now *Dixie* is heard and loved in both North as well as South, as it is one of the really popular songs of America in or out of the war. It has been pronounced by many the best light-hearted song that we have.

Written by a black-face minstrel who was a white man, loved by Abraham Lincoln and by many of the Northern soldiers, albeit it was one of the battle songs of the Confederacy, originating in the North and appropriated as a war ballad by the South, the rival for a time of even *Yankee Doodle, Dixie* is one of the few musical compositions that have outlived the Southern Confederacy.

Authorities disagree over the derivation of the name "Dixie." Of this much we are sure. Dixie, or Dixie's Land is a term which came to be identified with the South and Southern institutions just before and during the Civil War.

Previous to the advent of the song, the term was not in universal use by Southerners, although, whenever it was used, the term Dixie Land indicated the states south of the Mason and Dixon Line.

As far back as 1763, two English surveyors, Charles Mason and Jeremiah Dixon, were employed by Lord Baltimore and William Penn to establish the boundary line between Maryland and Pennsylvania. Most historians say that Dixie Land gradually grew out of Dixon's Land.

Another possible origin of the word Dixie, though not widely credited, is linked with the ten-dollar bills issued by the Citizens' Bank of Louisiana. During the 1850s this bank was considered the most stable in New Orleans, widely known through its innovation of accepting drafts drawn upon any bank in the country (contrary to the usual procedure which required presentation of a check at the particular bank upon which it was drawn). This practice appealed particularly to freight shippers in the Mississippi River trade, for they could present all their accumulated checks to the Citizens' Bank for a single payment while their boats were loading or unloading in New Orleans.

Naturally the many thousands of dollars paid out were distributed far and wide throughout the Mississippi River Valley by the steamboat men in payment for fuel, wharf-boat dues, supplies, wages, and port charges. These notes were kept in constant circulation and they became better known than those of any bank in the South.

Because of the extensive Creole patronage—the institution was also known as La Banque des Citoyens de la Louisiane—its notes were printed in both English and French. The denominations were therefore indicated as five, *cinq;* ten, *dix;* twenty, *vingt;* fifty, *cinquante;* one hundred, *cent;* one thousand, *mille.* For some unexplained reason, the ten-dollar bills, with the word *dix* prominent on both front and back, were the most popular denominations. The expression "a Dixie note" or a note from the "Dixie bank" therefore became very popular. A common and universal expression used by the rivermen when leaving from the up-river country for New Orleans was, "We're going South after Dixies," or going down to Dixie Land. Gradually the Southern country began to be known along the river ports as "Dixie Land" because so much money came from it. Some historians claim that from this beginning the word eventually became synonymous with the South everywhere.

Still another account, though one that seems farfetched, tells of a man named Dix, a slaveowner who had a large farm on Long Island, managed like a Southern plantation. He treated his many Negroes kindly and paid them well, so much so that Dix's land became a synonym for kindness to slaves. But when Abolition sentiment became strong, Mr. Dix was forced to give up his farm and ship his slaves to the Southern states, where they were not as well treated and had to work harder. They looked back at their old home with longing, wishing they were back in Dix's (Dixie's) land.

The composer of *Dixie,* Daniel Decatur Emmett, was

born in Mount Vernon, Ohio, on October 29, 1815, the son of the village blacksmith. His family were all locally well-known amateur musicians, hence it was natural that at an early age young Dan showed a talent for music, and he became an excellent fiddle and banjo player before he reached his teens. When he was sixteen he ran away to join a traveling circus, his act being to present songs of his own composition, with banjo accompaniment, in the Spalding & Rogers and the Oscar Brown circuses.

Later, with three stranded musicians, he traveled widely, singing and playing the banjo and violin. One night in a little town in New York state, Emmett blacked his hands and face with burnt cork and sang an old plantation song, accompanying himself on his banjo. Then his companions, faces also blackened, sang, danced, and played. So warm was their reception that they added jokes to their act, and their style of entertainment began to be popular. Prior to this time little show companies and circuses had carried with them educated Negroes to sing, dance, and entertain in plantation style. But after Emmett's debut as a black-face minstrel, the stage career of the genuine Negro was at an end. The day of the burnt-cork minstrel had dawned.

Emmett was so successful that in 1842 he and his three companions formed the Virginia Minstrels, the first black-face minstrel company in the United States. To the burnt cork, they added a combination of white trousers, striped calico shirt and blue swallowtail coat, which eventually became the trademark of all minstrels. After appearances in New York and Boston, the troupe tried their luck in

England, but the English did not seem to be amused by such strange antics and the engagement was not a success.

Returning to New York, Emmett earned a living as a musician in brass bands, for he found that during his absence abroad many competitive minstrel troupes had sprung up and copied his performance style. In 1858 he joined the Dan Bryant Minstrels, in which he both composed and performed comic songs and plantation Negro "walk-arounds." The latter were the songs sung at the end of the show as a solo performer walked around the stage.

One Saturday night in 1859, the manager of the company stopped him after a somewhat unsuccessful performance. The attendance had been meager all week. The numbers seemed to have gone stale, and applause was unenthusiastic and feeble.

"Dan, I must have a fresh tune. Can't you compose a new walk-around, something lively in the git-up-and-git style? Make it lively, something the bands will play and the boys will whistle in the streets. I'll expect it on Monday morning at rehearsal."

"That's a big order, Mr. Bryant," said Emmett, "but I'll see what I can do."

"You better have it by then, or—well, you'll wish you were in Dixie."

Sunday was cold and wet, and Dan sat in the kitchen without any inspiration. He walked to the window and looked out. A cold wind was whining, and Emmett was carried back to the time when as a boy he was traveling with the little circuses. The performers and Negro roustabouts always wished they were in Dixie Land when the cold weather came in the North.

When his wife Catherine came into the room, he said, "What a morning! I wish I was in Dixie."

"You show people," she said, "you keep talking about being in Dixie. What does it mean?"

"Well," he replied, "it's a common expression. When it's cold we yearn to be south of the Mason and Dixon Line, or in Dixie, where the weather is fair and mild. When things aren't going well where you are, you wish you were in Dixie—in Dixie—in Dixie."

This was the magical moment. "Suddenly," he later told a reporter, "I jumped up and sat down at the table to work. In less than an hour I had the first verse and chorus. After that, it was easy. When my wife returned, I sang it for her. 'It's all finished now except the name. What shall I call it?' 'Why, call it I Wish I Was in Dixie Land,' she said." And so it was.

At the rehearsal the next day, Mrs. Bryant, wife of the manager, expressed her fears that the first stanza might offend the religious-minded in the audience, so it was never used, though Emmett sometimes included it in souvenir copies:

Dis worl' was made in jiss six days,
An' finished up in various ways;
  Look away! Look away! Look away! Dixie Land!
Dey den made Dixie trim and nice,
But Adam called it "paradise,"
  Look away! Look away! Look away! Dixie Land!

The Negro dialect seemed to add to the lightness of the song and the brightness of the air permitted the performer to make a complete walk-around during each verse. The words, of course, were completely without any sense.

The song was so successful that Bryant gave Emmett a bonus of five dollars. *Dixie* was adopted at once by various other bands of touring minstrels who, in payment of a fee of five dollars, sang and danced it in all parts of the country.

Emmett sold the publication rights outright to the New York firm of Peters for the sum of five hundred dollars, all that he ever received for it after most of the current minstrel companies had purchased the rights of perform- ance. The song was issued under the title *I Wish I Was in Dixie Land.*

The first performance in the Southern states appears to have been in Charleston, South Carolina, in December, 1860, during the exciting and tense days before the state's withdrawal from the Union, when secession sentiment was at its peak. Rumsey and Newcomb's minstrel troupe played to crowded audiences for a week, with the *Dixie* walk-around as the climax. Since the local military bands had repudiated all the national airs connected with the North, they now needed new martial marching music, and *Dixie* seemed to fill the bill admirably.

But it was in New Orleans that *Dixie* was first accepted as a Southern war song. In March, 1861, after Louisiana had seceded, the theatrical troupe of Mrs. John Wood was opening in *Pocahontas* at the Varieties Theatre. The last scene was a Zouave drill and march, and Carlo Patti, brother of Adelina Patti, was the orchestra leader. At a preliminary rehearsal, the leader was at a loss as to what air he might use as the climax of the show. He tried several, and *Dixie* won the approval of the entire company.

At the first evening performance, as the last number, the gaudily dressed Zouaves marched onstage, led by Miss Susan Denim singing *I Wish I Was in Dixie*. The audience went wild with delight, and demanded seven encores. From that evening *Dixie* was the favorite song of the Confederacy. As war sentiment grew, the South began to apply the words of the song to its cause, recognizing themselves as a separate people occupying their own territory, Dixie Land. They therefore resolved to live and die in this beloved Dixie.

P. P. Werlein, a New Orleans publisher, had received a Northern copy of *Dixie* from Billy Newcomb, the minstrel who had paid five dollars for performance rights and had introduced the song in Charleston and other cities farther south. Werlein wrote to the composer to secure the Southern copyright, but with the declaration of war he decided not to wait for an answer, pirated it, and published the song in thousands of copies without any payment whatever to Emmett.

Just as *John Brown's Body* spread through the North, so from New Orleans *Dixie* spread throughout the newly formed Confederacy, where the soldiers took it up, sang it in camp and on the march and even charged in battle and died to its melody. Southern versemakers used it for every occasion—for rallying, volunteering, and to speed their soldiers to the front.

The Daughters of the Confederacy once uncovered twenty-two different Southern versions, and Elliott Shapiro has recorded thirty-nine, both Union and Confederate, issued between 1860 and 1864.

The only other words fitted to the tune which had much success were those composed by General Albert Pike of Arkansas, who published his version under the title *The War Song of Dixie,* popularly known as *Pike's Dixie.* The words, however, did not lend themselves to the bright air:

> Southrons, hear your country call you!
> Up! lest worse than death befall you!
> To arms! To arms! To arms! In Dixie!
> Lo, all the beacon-fires are lighted,
> Let all hearts be now united!
> To arms! To arms! To arms! In Dixie!

The Northerners were reluctant to have such a stirring song become sole Southern property, so the New York *Commercial Advertiser* editorially stated: "Whenever *Dixie* is produced, the pen drops from the fingers of the plodding clerk, the spectacles from the nose and the paper from the hands of the merchant, the needle from the nimble digits of the maid and matron, and all go hobbling, bobbling in tune with the magical music. Won't someone set it to words of Union sentiment?" Northern versions poured forth, but none was successful, for the North was *not* Dixie Land, and never could be. The Confederacy had irrevocably established the song as her own.

The song was played at Montgomery, Alabama, when the Confederate States of America was provisionally established. At the inauguration of Jefferson Davis as President of the permanent Confederacy, on February 22, 1862, the program was so arranged that the band led off with *Dixie* just as he started from the Old Exchange Hotel toward the Capitol building in Richmond. This was equivalent to its official adoption as the national song.

Dixie was a favorite of President Lincoln. When he was at City Point, Virginia, aboard the *River Queen* on April 8, 1865, immediately after the surrender at Appomattox, he was serenaded by a headquarters military band. He asked the Marquis de Chambrun, who was present as an observer, if he had ever heard the rebel song *Dixie*. The Frenchmen had not, so the President continued, "That tune is now Federal property and it is good to show the rebels that, with us in power, they will be free to hear it again," whereupon he requested the surprised musicians to play it.

Back in Washington the next day, a crowd of joyous citizens celebrating the end of the war gathered on the lawn of the White House. The United States Military Band played many of the Union airs which had been popular during the war.

Members of the throng called for the President to say a few words. Rising in the balcony and bowing to the sea of heads in front, he spoke to them.

"Gentlemen, I cannot make a speech tonight. I rather feel like hearing music. I want to hear my favorite old tune, *Dixie*. I always did love *Dixie,* and the Attorney-General says that we may have it, for *Dixie,* gentlemen, is now our own by right of conquest."

After a rousing performance of the tune, the band

played *Yankee Doodle, My Maryland,* and *The Star-Spangled Banner. Dixie* had returned to the Union.

Though a Northerner, Dan Emmett was sometimes accused of disloyalty and marked as a Confederate sympathizer because of Southern acceptance of his song. Part of this attack was due to the fact that his father was a Virginian, his mother a Marylander. Some, like the editor of a Maine newspaper, even went so far as to suggest that he be tried as a traitor! All this opposition failed to consider that the song was written two years before the war began and had enjoyed a national reputation in both North and South wherever minstrel shows were performed.

When Bryant's troupe disbanded in 1865, Emmett moved to Chicago, where he earned his living as a musician. He lost all his possessions in the great fire of 1871. In 1882, when he was almost seventy years old, a number of Chicago theater managers organized a large benefit performance honoring him as the father of black-face minstrelsy. The proceeds were sent to him at his small farm in Mount Vernon, Ohio, to which he had returned in 1878.

There he led a quiet life, content with his memories, his neighbors unaware that a famous man was among them. The Actors' Fund granted him a small pension of ten dollars a week, which enabled him, in those days, to live simply but comfortably.

But when Al G. Fields visited the town in 1895 and offered the old man a contract with his minstrel company, the lure of footlights and burnt cork caused him to return to the stage. For several years, though in his eighties, Dan Emmett, still physically active, trouped again, performing his walk-around, always ending the performance with *Dixie*. This, he said, was the high point in his life, for he again was a wildly applauded star. During this tour his dressing room was robbed and the original manuscript of the song, yellowed with age, which he had intended donating to a Southern library or museum, was stolen.

Though best known for *Dixie*, Emmett wrote scores of other popular minstrel tunes, including *Old Dan Tucker, Jordan Is a Hard Road to Travel, The Road to Richmond*, and *Early in the Morning*. He popularized folk tunes of obscure origin such as *Root Hog or Die, Turkey in the Straw*, and *Blue Tail Fly*. He estimated that during his career he had composed over two hundred walk-arounds which he never published.

Dan Emmett died on June 28, 1904, and was buried in Mound View Cemetery in Mount Vernon. The inscription on the red granite tombstone over his grave reads: "His song inspired the courage and devotion of the Southern people and now thrills the hearts of a reunited nation."

The town is filled with reminders of its famous resident. On the little white house where he was born is a plaque reading, "The birthplace of Daniel Decatur Emmett, 1815–1904, author of 'Dixie' and founder of minstrelsy."

Mount Vernon also has a Dan Emmett Elementary School, an Emmett Drive, Decatur Drive and a Dan Emmett Grange. In the center of the town is a bronze plaque mounted on a boulder, the gift of the Ohio division of the United Daughters of the Confederacy. On the hundredth anniversary of the writing of the song, in October, 1959, Mount Vernon had a three-day celebration. At that time Congressman Robert W. Levering of Ohio suggested that the Post Office Department should issue a special stamp in honor of the composer, rejecting the idea that the song belonged to the South exclusively.

In 1915, *The Confederate Veteran* instituted a campaign for new words of greater dignity, "more in the spirit of the Confederacy," patriotic words to be sung to the glorious air. But no suitable versions were received. The original words in Negro dialect are so much a part of the song that any others have always seemed out of place.

No matter what one thinks about the musical quality of *Dixie,* no one can dispute the fact that the song was a tremendous power during the Civil War and continued to be a favorite in days of peace.

☆☆☆☆☆☆☆☆☆

Maryland,
My Maryland

Maryland, My Maryland

Hark to an exiled son's appeal,
  Maryland!
My Mother State! To thee I kneel,
  Maryland!
For life and death, for woe and weal,
Thy peerless chivalry reveal,
And gird thy beauteous limbs with steel,
  Maryland, my Maryland!

Thou wilt not cower in the dust,
  Maryland!
Thy beaming sword shall never rust,
  Maryland!
Remember Carroll's sacred trust,
Remember Howard's warlike thrust,
And all thy slumberers with the just,
  Maryland, my Maryland!

Thou wilt not yield the vandal toll,
  Maryland!
Thou wilt not crook to his control,
  Maryland!

Better the fire upon thee roll,
Better the shot, the blade, the bowl,
Than crucifixion of the soul,
  Maryland, my Maryland! *

JAMES RYDER RANDALL

1861

---

* *The complete poem contains nine stanzas.*

CHAPTER 10

Maryland, My Maryland

The opening of the Civil War, preceded by the secession of
seven states of the "deep" South—South Carolina, Mississippi, Florida, Alabama, Georgia, Louisiana, and Texas
in the months between December, 1860, and February,
1861—was a time of anxiety in the North and jubilation
in the South.

As events moved relentlessly towards the final declaration
of war immediately after the attack on Fort Sumter and its
fall on April 14, 1861, the citizens of at least five border
states, those most closely linked to the North by geography
and their attitudes toward the institution of slavery—Maryland, Delaware, Virginia, Tennessee, and Kentucky—found
themselves sharply divided in their loyalties.

Should they remain within the Union, or should they
ally themselves with the provisional government of the
Confederate States of America, formed in the previous
February? The eventual decision was not one to be made

lightly, for the wrong choice might well be the difference between survival and ruin.

In no state was this decision more difficult than in Maryland, linked as it was to the Southern way of life and ideals. From a Union viewpoint, the loyalty of the state was an absolute necessity, for through it must pass all the troops and supplies sent by the upper Atlantic and New England states for the defense of the capital city and to an eventual battle line in the most northern of the truly Southern states, Virginia, which was to secede on April 17 and would probably become the principal battleground.

Following the declaration of war and Lincoln's call for 75,000 troops from the loyal states, a wave of enthusiasm resulted in the almost magical enlistment of thousands of volunteers, eager to be off for what they thought at the time would be a quelling of the rebellion in a few weeks.

In these mid-April days, all Northern soldiers must pass through the city of Baltimore en route to Washington. In the city, troops had to change trains by boarding horse-drawn cars for a ride across town from the President Street Station to the Camden Street Station.

For a week after the fall of Fort Sumter the tempers of the pro-Southern citizens of Baltimore were at a dangerous boiling point over the invasion of their soil. On Friday, April 19, troops of the Sixth Massachusetts Volunteers made the passage between stations on Pratt Street, which was lined with infuriated citizens bearing Confederate flags. Nine cars filled with Union soldiers passed unharmed, but the brake of the tenth car inopportunely locked, and it ground to a stop.

The anti-Northerners began to stone the troops, and a few trigger-happy Southern patriots shot at the hated Union soldiers, a fire which was promptly returned. The result of this riot was the death of four soldiers and twenty citizens, with thirty-six of the military and many Baltimoreans wounded. Though the insurrection was put down, and Union soldiers continued to pass through the city without interference, all Maryland seethed with unrest and violence. For a long time the state's loyalty to the Union hung in the balance.

The citizens of the Southern states awaited the outcome in understandable suspense. There was a man in Louisiana, a former Marylander, who found it impossible to remain silent. Twenty-two-year-old James Ryder Randall had left his native Baltimore several years previously and was at the time a teacher at a small but richly endowed private institution, Poydras College, Louisiana, near Point Coupée, 120 miles north of New Orleans. He considered himself a loyal Southerner and was naturally a strong supporter of secession.

Following the newspapers closely as the storms of war gathered force, he had, in his own words, "reached a fever pitch of excitement." When he read the account of the Baltimore riot in the April twentieth issue of the New Orleans *Daily Delta,* the war suddenly became personal to him. The list of casualties included one of his former schoolmates. He was familiar with every foot of ground where the altercation had taken place. The uprising in his home town, he wrote later, "set my Southern blood to fever heat."

Though far away and unable to participate in the strug-

gle, his excitement increased, and he found himself im-
pelled to action. He could not sleep the night after reading
about the riot in the New Orleans newspaper. Later he
wrote, "My nerves were all unstrung, and I could not dismiss what I had read from my mind. About midnight I
arose, lit a candle and went to my desk. Some powerful
spirit seemed to possess me, and almost involuntarily I
proceeded to write the verses of *My Maryland*. I remember
that the ideas appeared to take shape first as music in the
brain, some wild air."

"The whole poem was dashed off rapidly when once begun," he recalled. "It was not composed in cold blood,
but under what may be called a conflagration of the senses.
I was stirred to a desire for some way [of] linking my name
to that of my native state."

Once they were on paper, Randall found it unnecessary
to make any changes in his verses. After reading the poem
to his students in class the next morning, signing it "R"
and dating it Point Coupée, April 26, 1861, he sent it to the
editor of the *Delta*, in which it appeared in the issue of
May 1.

After this initial appearance, the poem was widely reprinted throughout the South. Baltimore was occupied by
Union soldiers after the riot. Even so, Confederate sympathies were not lessened, and censorship was not yet im-
posed upon pro-Southern newspapers. From one of the
journals arriving in Baltimore by packet boat, the editor
of *The South* copied *Maryland, My Maryland,* and printed
it in the issue of May 31. Soon thereafter it was reprinted
and distributed in thousands of broadside copies.

The home of the Cary family in Baltimore was a center

of pro-Confederate activities, and was the scene of many a sewing circle and the packing of boxes of clothing and supplies to be forwarded secretly to the front in Virginia. An amateur singing group met regularly in the parlors of the Cary mansion. Jennie, one of three daughters, all well-known belles of local society, was in charge of the June meeting of the glee club. In vain she searched through her songbooks seeking some new and thrilling song which had not yet been sung and re-sung. The current Confederate rallying songs had not yet reached Baltimore.

"I'm tired of the sentimental songs. I want something to make the rafters of this house ring!" she told her sister Hetty.

Bringing out the recent issue of *The South,* Hetty showed Randall's poem to her sister, saying "Here's your rousing song. All you need is a tune."

In a Yale College songbook, Jennie discovered *Lauriger Horatius,* a favorite song of German origin. Under the title *Tannenbaum,* written in 1824, the tune had become popular as a Christmas carol. The members of the glee club would surely be familiar with it.

Jennie needed only to add the alternate phrases of "My Maryland" to adapt Randall's poem to the meter of the tune. The song was sung rousingly by the choristers, and, as Jennie had hoped, the rafters rang.

Shortly after this first performance, Jennie Cary met a local publisher on the street. He asked her if she had read the poem. She told him of its adaptation to the German tune, and even invited him to hear it sung by a group of local girls at a sewing bee. But he was afraid to publish it for fear of reprisal by the occupation forces, who had not taken kindly to its appearance in *The South* and the many reprints.

Rebecca Nicholson, the granddaughter of the Judge Joseph Nicholson who had aided Francis Scott Key in publishing *The Star-Spangled Banner* nearly fifty years before, took it to the local music publishing firm of Miller & Beecham. With a few simple musical changes made by an editor, the song was printed with a note "Written by a Baltimorean in Louisiana." The composition spread like wildfire, and its publishers were punished by having their business suspended. *Maryland, My Maryland* immediately became a rallying song of the Southern cause.

Though the composition quickly found its way south, it was not published there until 1862, when Randall sold the publication rights to a New Orleans firm, A. E. Blackmar, for one hundred dollars. The poet's name appeared for the first time on these copies. This was the only payment he ever received for his poem.

The Cary sisters were also responsible for the introduction of the song into the Confederate Army. When their pro-Southern activities made it necessary for them to leave Baltimore, they ran the blockade across the Potomac River into Virginia in the late summer of 1861. The recent Confederate victory at Manassas (Bull Run) was everywhere being celebrated at the time.

General P. T. Beauregard had heard of their contributions to the Southern war effort, and invited Jennie and Hetty to visit his headquarters. After an inspection trip over the battlefield, they remained in camp, and were serenaded by the band of the New Orleans Washington Artillery. As a gesture of thanks, Jennie, standing at the door of her tent, sang *Maryland, My Maryland*. Hetty later wrote, "This, I believe, was the birth of the song in the Confederate Army. The refrain was speedily caught up and tossed back to us from hundreds of rebel throats. . . . There surged forth from the throng a wild shout, 'We *will* break her chains! Maryland shall be free!' "

At first the song shared equal popularity with *Dixie*. But when Maryland cast its lot with the Union and Lee's first invasion of the state failed, it was gradually dropped by the Confederates, and seldom heard thereafter in Southern camps. Union poets attempted to adapt the poem and tune to their own purposes, but it was so completely Southern in spirit that these versions failed.

In spite of the fact that James Ryder Randall composed over fifty other poems, none rivaled *My Maryland*, though he wrote another Confederate rallying song, *There's Life in the Old Land Yet!* He was a journalist in Augusta, Georgia, and for a time he lived in Washington as a correspondent. Later from the 1880s to 1903, he was secretary to two members of Congress from his adopted state, Georgia. He had enlisted in the Confederate Army, but was immediately mustered out for medical reasons. Married shortly after the war, he named one of his eight children Maryland in honor of his native state.

His prominence as a Catholic layman caused the University of Notre Dame to honor him with a Doctor of Laws degree. He died in Augusta on January 14, 1908.

Long after his death his beloved native state in 1939

made the composition its official song. A year before, a bronze plaque honoring James Ryder Randall was placed on a large oak tree at Point Coupée, on the site of Poydras College, which had been destroyed by fire in 1881. Randall's name thus still lives as the author of one of the Confederacy's most rousing songs.

Today it is difficult to realize the attraction of the song for both the Marylanders and other Southerners of the time. But the meaning of the song was not limited to the state, for it represented a call to arms for all the Confederate states who were pledged to resist Northern "vandals."

Maryland, My Maryland has often been called the *Marseillaise* of the Confederacy. "What Rouget de Lisle was to France," one writer has said, "Randall was to the Confederacy. What the *Marseillaise* was when the entire French nation went mad, *My Maryland* was when the Southern people threw themselves into the tumultous horror of our Civil War. . . . It stirred a fever in the blood. It was a bugle-call, a cry to arms, a battle-shout all in one. . . ."

Many still consider it the best poem to come out of the war on the Confederate side, having no peer in its stirring appeals to patriotism, pride, and valor. Oliver Wendell Holmes was one of its most devoted admirers, writing, "I always *felt* rather than thought there was a genuine ring and a life-like spirit in the lyric."

The nine-stanza song was one of the longest of the popular Civil War compositions, but only three stanzas are generally sung in modern times. Like many another of our national songs, the music is of foreign origin.

A prime test of a truly great poem is that it outlives the

period in which it was written and the occasion which prompted its composition. *Maryland, My Maryland* meets this test. Its stirring words still have the power to thrill, a century later.

☆☆☆☆☆☆☆☆☆☆

The Battle-Cry
of Freedom

The Battle-Cry of Freedom

Yes, we'll rally round the flag, boys, we'll rally once
    again,
    Shouting the battle-cry of Freedom;
We will rally from the hillside, we'll gather from the
    plain,
    Shouting the battle-cry of Freedom.

CHORUS

The Union forever, hurrah, boys, hurrah!
Down with the traitor and up with the star;
While we rally round the flag, boys, rally once again,
Shouting the battle-cry of Freedom.

We are springing to the call of our brothers gone
    before,
    Shouting the battle-cry of Freedom;
And we'll fill the vacant ranks with a million freemen
    more,
    Shouting the battle-cry of Freedom.

We will welcome to our numbers the loyal, true and
    brave,
    Shouting the battle-cry of Freedom;

And altho' they may be poor, not a man shall be a
    slave,
  Shouting the battle-cry of Freedom.

So we're springing to the call from the East and from
    the West,
  Shouting the battle-cry of Freedom;
And we'll hurl the rebel crew from the land we love
    the best,
  Shouting the battle-cry of Freedom.
1861

GEORGE F. ROOT

CHAPTER 11

The Battle-Cry of Freedom

There has never been an emergency in American history without a man or woman to meet it. Some may try and fail, but the right person to perform the needed service is sure to appear at the right time. This is true of composers and poets as well as politicians and generals.

George Frederick Root was such a man from the very beginning to long past the end of the Civil War. As the most productive Union musician of the period, he wrote more than forty songs of all types, on many different subjects. He rallied support for the Northern cause, spurred volunteering and enlistments, and urged patriotism and loyalty. He pictured the loneliness of the soldier and the prisoner, expressed the feelings of the fighting man before and after the battle, and depicted the grief, loneliness, and anxiety of the families at home.

In his autobiography he admitted that he was affected by any and every incident or feeling which moved his loyal fellow men, saying, "That I was able to express their emotions so well is due entirely to the fact that I felt myself one of them and what *I* felt appeared to be exactly what *they* felt. What has been called my 'inspiration' was merely the result of this kinship in those stirring, anxious and often unhappy times."

Lincoln himself once wrote to Root to thank him for his contribution to the Union war effort, saying, "Through your many songs you have done more than a hundred generals and a thousand orators. If you could not shoulder a musket in the defense of your country, you certainly have served her through songs."

Unlike most composers of our songs of patriotism, George F. Root's claims to distinction do not rest on a single composition. Any of at least four of his songs—*The Battle-Cry of Freedom, Just Before the Battle, Mother, The Vacant Chair,* and *Tramp, Tramp, Tramp*—would entitle him to a place in the front rank of those musicians who came forward in times of stress with compositions to thrill and move the people.

When George Frederick Root was born in Sheffield, Massachusetts, on August 30, 1820, he was given the Christian names of the great Handel, the favorite composer of his mother, who was an excellent singer. The young lad possessed inherited musical ability, and by the time he was eight years old and the family had moved to North Reading, he had mastered the flute well enough to play it in church. His mother encouraged his musical interest, and when he had reached the age of thirteen he was able to play by ear that many different instruments, one for each year he had lived! The family of eight children formed a self-contained chorus which the young lad conducted.

In those days pianos in homes were a luxury, and for lessons one had usually to go to conservatories or teachers in large cities. By the time he was eighteen, the youth had determined to make music his career. He therefore began to work for A. N. Johnson in Boston, for a wage of three dollars a week, board, and piano lessons. In return he was expected to tend the fire, sweep the studio, and take charge when Mr. Johnson was absent. His teacher was associated with Lowell Mason, the man who had introduced *America* in Boston and who was prominent in New England music circles. Root learned to play the organ as well as piano so quickly that he soon became Mason's assistant organist and rehearsal pianist. He also accumulated valuable experience in directing choruses and church choirs.

These many activities brought young Root to the attention of Jacob Abbott, author of the then-popular Rollo books, who took the youth to New York City as an instructor in his music school. During a fifteen-year period thereafter, Root worked with teachers of school music and thus laid the groundwork for lifelong work in elementary-school music. It was during this time that he began composing. The firm of Hall and Sons published several of his songs under the pseudonym of George Friedrich Würzel, the German word for Root. *Hazel Dell* and *Rosalie, the Prairie Flower* immediately became popular.

The royalties from these two compositions alone made him financially independent. He had realized that school teachers knew very little about music. Through Mason's influence the subject had been added to the course of study in the Massachusetts public schools, but the teachers were untrained. Accordingly, Mr. Root returned to his home in North Reading, and began conducting what he called Normal Music Institutes, the first being held in 1852. These were three-month sessions for school teachers, in which he gave simple instruction in music-teaching methods.

So successful was this innovation that his services began to be in demand at state and local teachers' conventions as far west as Ohio, Michigan, Indiana, and Illinois. Recognizing the greater opportunities in the Middle West, Root settled in Chicago in 1858, and established the music publishing firm of Root and Cady, in partnership with his brother Towner and C. M. Cady, later being joined by another brother William.

The firm of Root and Cady decided to concentrate on issuing music for schools. George F. Root began the compilation of the first of his songbooks and song collections for children, an occupation which was to continue throughout his life. He eventually published over a dozen.

But when the guns at Fort Sumter turned the attention of all Northerners to the war effort in 1861, he began to add to this work the composition and publication of war songs.

News of the declaration of war was still being shouted on the streets of Chicago when Root had completed *The First Gun Is Fired!*, the first Union song of the Civil War. Issued within ten days in both broadside and sheet-music form, the chorus called upon all loyal Northerners to

Arise! arise! arise!
And gird ye for the fight;
And let our watch-word ever be
"May God protect the right!"

Though Lincoln's first call for troops in April had met with great success, more soldiers were needed. On May 3, 1861, the President therefore issued an appeal for forty additional army regiments (22,000 men) and 18,000 seamen for the navy.

When the news reached Chicago that afternoon, Root was resting on a sofa in his brother's home. Here was another challenge. "Immediately a song started in my mind," he later recorded, "words and music together:

Yes, we'll rally round the flag, boys, we'll rally once again,
Shouting the battle-cry of Freedom.

I thought it out that afternoon, and wrote it the next morning at the store." The ink was hardly dry when the Lumbard brothers, the great singers of the war, came in for something to sing at a war meeting that was to be held immediately in the courthouse square just opposite. They went through the new song once, and then hastened to the steps of the courthouse, followed by a crowd that had gathered while the practice was going on. Then Jules Lumbard's magnificent voice gave out the verse, and his brother Frank's trumpet tones led the refrain

The Union, forever, hurrah, boys, hurrah!

By the time they had reached the fourth verse, a thousand voices were joining in the chorus.

Only a few days afterward, a huge war rally was held in Union Square in New York City. The Hutchinson family, another singing group that traveled widely throughout the war, opened the meeting by singing *The Battle-Cry of Freedom*. The throng of listeners were roused to the highest pitch of feeling. The song was repeated again and again, and proved an immediate hit.

The Battle-Cry of Freedom appeared at the psychological moment, and its spread was rapid and phenomenal. Root sent the first published copy to his wife, who was then in North Reading. One of the favorite graduates of her husband's first course had just volunteered, and was in a nearby camp, so she visited him and gave him a copy of the new song as a going-away present. It was this music teacher turned soldier, James R. Murray, who was said to have introduced the tune into the ranks of the Union Army in Virginia.

Throughout the war the strains "We'll rally round the flag, boys" came from the throats of soldiers and citizens, for it possessed every quality necessary in a thrilling war song—a depth of feeling, a call to patriotism, a rallying of loyal men, and an assurance of success. It was often sung as the men marched into action, and many times its melody rose on the battlefield to stimulate courage.

The Battle-Cry of Freedom had particular appeal to the soldiers, for it was one of the earliest war songs to reach them. Easy to sing, the composition struck a responsive chord in the hearts of the rank and file of the army. The song was used in every theater of war, always giving a needed lift of spirit in good and bad times. In their memoirs, soldiers offered abundant testimony to its power and effect.

Morale in the Union Army at the close of 1862 was at a low point. The Army of the Cumberland had suffered a reverse at Perryville in October, and the Confederate invasion of Kentucky might still be successful. Exhausted from long marches, the soldiers were suffering a letdown after the heavy casualities of the Battle of Stones River or Murfreesboro in which the losses had been 13,000 out of the 41,000 troops engaged.

A young soldier reported what happened. "By a happy accident," he wrote, "the glee club which came down from Chicago a few days afterward sang *The Battle-Cry of Freedom* thrillingly. The effect was little short of miraculous. The tune put as much spirit and cheer into the army as a splendid victory. Day and night you could hear it by every camp fire and in every tent. Never shall I forget how these men rolled out the lines. I do not know whether Mr. Root ever knew what good work his song did for us there, but I hope so."

An officer who was in one of the battles during the siege of Vicksburg told of an Iowa regiment that went into the fight eight hundred strong and came out with a terrible loss of more than half their number. "But," he said, "the brave fellows who remained were waving their torn and powder-stained banner and singing, 'Yes, we'll rally round the flag, boys.' "

Reminiscences of soldiers mention the power of *The*

Battle-Cry of Freedom more often than any other song written during the desperate struggle.

In May, 1864, during the terrible Battle of the Wilderness, a Union brigade became exposed to a flank attack and were driven back in disorder with a heavy loss. They had retreated but a few hundred yards, however, when they reformed and again attacked the enemy. At that moment a gallant soldier of the 45th Pennsylvania Infantry began to shout, "We'll rally round the flag, boys." The refrain was caught up by the entire regiment and also by the soldiers immediately behind them in the line. The air was filled with smoke and the crackle of the burning underbrush, the pitiful cries of the wounded, the rattle of musketry, and the wild shouts of command. But above all rose the inspiring chorus "The Union forever, hurrah, boys, hurrah!"

As a piece of poetry, *The Battle-Cry of Freedom* may not possess great merit, but as an expression of patriotism it is beyond price. It had merit enough to give it enduring fame as a battle song, merit enough to inspire men to leave their homes and join the army in defense of the Union, and merit enough to be sung by ten thousand voices in the Republican convention of 1867 to arouse enthusiasm for the nomination of Ulysses S. Grant as a Presidential candidate.

Inspiration was to come to George Root many times after that May morning of 1861, always resulting in a song appropriate for the times. Composition was no task for him, for his experience in extemporizing tunes on the blackboard during his classes made it easy for him to produce a song almost on order.

His next major composition, *The Vacant Chair*, was in

an entirely different vein. Its appeal was to the civilians at home. Like many another youth, eighteen-year-old John William (Willie) Grout of Worcester, Massachusetts, had joined the army in the first flush of Civil War enthusiasm. He was stationed north of Washington in the fall of 1861, and expected to have his first furlough to return to his home for Thanksgiving. But he was wounded and drowned at the Battle of Ball's Bluff the last week in October, and at the dinner table on the holiday his chair, in its usual place, was left unoccupied.

A friend of the family, Henry S. Washburn, was so moved by the unspoken grief of the family and the memories the vacant chair evoked that he composed a poem in honor of Willie Grout. The refrain reflected the sorrow which was to come to many families:

> We shall meet, but we shall miss him,
> There will be one vacant chair;
> We shall linger to caress him
> When we breathe our evening prayer.

George F. Root set the words to fitting and moving music, and the song was published by his firm early in 1862. Coming in the first year of the war, it was destined to express the sentiments of many a family. *The Vacant Chair* became one of the most popular mourning ballads of the war, loved and sung in both North and South, for its sincere emotion was common to all families who had lost a son.

Root did not forget the soldier at the front facing an uncertain future which might mean wounds or even death.

In *Just Before the Battle, Mother,* published in 1863, he pictured the feelings of a young soldier on the eve of an engagement.

> Just before the battle, mother,
>   I am thinking most of you,
> While upon the field we're waiting
> With the enemy in view.
> Comrades brave are 'round me lying,
> Filled with thoughts of home and God,
> For well they know that on the morrow
>   Some will sleep beneath the sod.
>
> CHORUS
> Farewell, mother, you may never
> Press me to your breast again;
>   But, oh, you'll not forget me, mother,
>   If I'm numbered with the slain.

Since a quarter of a million Union soldiers were under eighteen, the legal age for enlistment in the army, it was natural that many would think of their mothers when danger was imminent.

The success of this song led Root to compose an equally popular companion piece, *Just After the Battle, Mother,* later in the same year. In this song he pictured the despair and loneliness of a wounded soldier lying on the battlefield awaiting the dawn after a bloody combat.

As the war lengthened, Root unceasingly poured out his melodies. When the Northern Copperheads raised loud objections to continuance of the war, the composer appealed to all loyal people, in *Stand Up for Uncle Sam, My Boys.*

By the late months of 1863, thousands of Union soldiers were being held captive in Confederate prisons, their plight stirring all Northerners. Root used this subject in three songs. The first, *Tramp, Tramp, Tramp,* was second only to *The Battle-Cry of Freedom* in popularity.

Root and Cady published a monthly magazine, *The Song Messenger,* which had a wide circulation among music teachers and musicians. The periodical, a sort of house organ, included articles on teaching, and served to introduce the music currently being issued by the firm. An annual New Year's extra always contained an unpublished song composed especially for the issue by Root. *Just Before the Battle, Mother* had been the song for 1862.

When the deadline for the 1863 extra approached, George Root was devoting all his time to the preparation of a series of school songbooks, and had postponed the composition of that year's song. His brother William reminded Root of the need for a new title, saying, "We must have a song or we cannot get out the issue in time for New Year's. Go right now and write it while it's on your mind."

Within two hours Root had produced *Tramp, Tramp, Tramp* and showed it to his brother. They played it over together. William's reaction was, "I must confess I don't think much of it, but it *may* do, in fact it *must* do. You have certainly written better numbers."

The song, subtitled *The Prisoner's Hope,* pictured a lonely and sick Union army captive whose only hope of liberation lay in the coming of the Northern forces to "open wide the iron door" and liberate him and his suffering comrades:

> In the prison cell I sit, thinking, mother dear, of you
>   And the bright and happy home so far away;
> And the tears they fill my eyes 'spite of all that I can do,
>   Though I try to cheer my comrades and be gay.

> CHORUS
> Tramp, tramp, tramp, the boys are marching,
> Cheer up, comrades, they will come;
> And beneath the starry flag we will breathe the air again
> Of the freeland of our own beloved home.

The subject was close to the hearts of the people. The expectation expressed in the words, however, was not to come true until much later, for prisoner exchange was slowed down and finally ceased. Many captives kept themselves alive by hopes for their liberation when the Union armies were penetrating further and further into the Southern states. Many of them were freed toward the end of the war when Sherman's army opened prison doors in the March to the Sea, pictured in Henry Clay Work's *Marching Through Georgia*.

With the subtitle *The Prisoner Free*, Root late in 1864 pictured this situation in *On, On, On, the Boys Came Marching* as a sequel to *Tramp, Tramp, Tramp:*

On, on, on, the boys came marching,
Like a grand majestic sea,

And they dashed away the guard from the heavy iron door,
And we stood beneath the starry banner, free!

Root did not fail to recognize the plight of the captives at Andersonville, Georgia, the most notorious of all Confederate prisons. The infamous story of Andersonville was one of the most unhappy of the war because of the high incidence of death, almost a fourth of the 50,000 prisoners dying in slightly over a year, due largely to malnutrition and disease. In *Starved in Prison* the usually gentle composer gave vent to the righteous indignation of his fellow Northerners at the continued news of these casualties.

George F. Root's final war songs in 1865 concerned the fall of Richmond, a song of mourning for President Lincoln, and an appeal to the defeated Southerners for forgiveness and friendliness.

After the war Root continued the Chicago publishing business, but it was wiped out in the disastrous fire of 1871, and was never re-established. His songs were thereafter published by John C. Church of Cincinnati, while he continued his activities in advancing the cause of public-school music.

He died on August 6, 1895, at the age of seventy-five. He left a legacy of songs which not only aroused patriotic sentiments but also were a force in the increasing recognition and acceptance of good music for young people in and out of school.

The fire of Root's great *Battle-Cry of Freedom* still burned after his death, offering proof again that a truly great song outlives the immediate circumstances which brought it to light.

On July 4, 1896, an audience of ten thousand people assembled in the Chicago Coliseum, the occasion being a benefit war song festival to raise funds for a monument in George F. Root's honor. Over two dozen of his songs were on the program. The city's foremost singers sang the solos, and one thousand school children the choruses. Jules Lumbard, now a white-haired veteran, who was the first to sing *The Battle-Cry of Freedom* thirty-five years before, sang it as the climax of the program, and every listener was thrilled anew by its power.

Luther Laflin Mills then delivered a brief address on the influence of Root's songs, saying: "The songs of George F. Root abide and will remain in the memories and voices of our people, not only as a reminder of the nation's heroic struggle for self-preservation, but as a constant, inspiring and educating force in maintaining and strengthening the lofty sentiments of American patriotism."

Charles A. Dana, editor of the New York *Sun*, who had been Secretary of War in Lincoln's cabinet, paid a fitting tribute to Root in the following year, when he said: "George Root did more to preserve the Union than a great many Brigadier-Generals, and quite as much as some brigades. His songs were a great force in the homes of the people as well as among the men in the field. They touched the chords of patriotism as they had never been touched before. His songs became the ruling sentiment of the American people, they were eloquent appeals for enlistment, and their power made millions 'rally round the flag.' "

✩✩✩✩✩✩✩✩✩

John Brown's Body

John Brown's Body

John Brown's body lies a-mouldering in the grave,
John Brown's body lies a-mouldering in the grave,
John Brown's body lies a-mouldering in the grave,
His soul is marching on!

CHORUS
Glory, glory, hallelujah!
Glory, glory, hallelujah!
Glory, glory, hallelujah!
His soul is marching on.

He's gone to be a soldier in the army of the Lord,
He's gone to be a soldier in the army of the Lord,
He's gone to be a soldier in the army of the Lord,
His soul is marching on!

John Brown's knapsack is strapped on his back, etc.
His soul is marching on!

His pet lambs will meet him on the way, etc.
They go marching on!

They will hang Jeff Davis to a sour apple tree, etc.
       As they march along!

Now, three rousing cheers for the Union, etc.
       As we are marching on!

ATTRIBUTED TO VARIOUS AUTHORS

1861

CHAPTER 12

John Brown's Body

In times of national peril the people become attached to songs of noble patriotic sentiments. However, the soldiers who are fighting the war seem less inclined to take as their own the grand airs, and often content themselves with rollicking songs which can be loudly sung to the cadence of the march.

The words of the songs best loved by the soldiers rarely make sense, yet they serve the essential purpose of lifting the spirits of the fighting men. The nonsense of *Yankee Doodle*'s words appealed to the men who fought for freedom and liberty during the American Revolution, and the rhythm of its music as played on the fife, drum, or penny whistle was irresistible. Though written by an Ohio man, *Dixie* was taken over by the soldiers of the Confederacy as their own. Similarly, though its air was a Southern camp-meeting tune, *John Brown's Body*, sometimes called *Glory*,

Hallelujah! or the *John Brown Song,* became the favorite marching song of the Union Army.

John Brown was and still is an enigma in American history. At a time when anti-slavery sentiment was growing by leaps and bounds in the Northern states and Abolitionists were taking action, through the underground railroad, to supplement their beliefs and words, this fanatic who claimed to be led by visions and prayers, became a legendary figure. During twenty years he dreamed of freedom for the slaves and died trying to make his dream a reality.

Using his sons as a nucleus, this Connecticut-born man was able to gather together a band of fifteen or twenty adventurers who presently began to make his name a terror to his opponents in Kansas, where he settled in 1855. He was fully persuaded that he was God's messenger sent to destroy slavery, and it was in the struggle which the Free State men were making for the control of the new territory that he first appeared as a public character. Working from his headquarters at Osawatomie in Miami County, with arms furnished by Abolitionist sympathizers throughout the Northern states, he made a heroic stand against an overwhelming force of slave-holding invaders from Missouri.

A concentrated effort was being made to extend slavery to the new territories, and John Brown played his part in the successful contest which kept it out of the territory of Kansas. Active in guerrilla warfare, he did not shrink from murder when he felt it was necessary. So completely devoted was he to his ideal that he sacrificed three sons in the struggle: one shot to death, one dead from wounds, a third made insane from torture. His passionate hatred of slavery, intensified by his personal and family sacrifices and a year's border fighting, led him to put thought into even greater action late in 1857, when he began to plan a massed invasion into the South to free the slaves.

He laid the groundwork in a trip throughout the Northern states, appealing for arms and supplies for his dream project. In Boston he met Julia Ward Howe, whose husband was also an active and prominent Abolitionist. She once described Brown as a middle-aged man, with hair and short beard of amber color, streaked with gray. "He looked a Puritan of the Puritans, forceful, concentrated and self-contained," she wrote. The impression he made upon her was so indelible that it was closely linked to her composition of *The Battle Hymn of the Republic* several years later, when the Civil War came.

As a surveyor during his youth, John Brown had become well acquainted with the Allegheny Mountains; he knew the special points which could be held by a hundred men against a thousand. God told him, he claimed, that the area lying between the slave states of Maryland and Virginia was the predestined refuge for a body of fugitive slaves. When he was ready to take action on his plan, he chose the town of Harper's Ferry, Virginia, where the Potomac and Shenandoah Rivers met, as the scene for his demonstration.

He had often declared "Give a slave a pike, and you make him a man." Mistakenly, as it turned out, he conceived the idea that, upon a certain signal, the slaves from many surrounding plantations would rally to him in such numbers that he and they would become masters of the situation, with little or no bloodshed.

Before moving to a farm in Maryland, five miles from Harper's Ferry, on the Fourth of July, 1859, John Brown had grown the flowing spadelike beard and heavy mustache which was to aid his disguise under an assumed name. For several months he secretly collected rifles, revolvers, ammunition, pikes, blankets, tents, and supplies for a campaign, which was to take the form of the guerrilla warfare with which he had become so familiar in Kansas.

Sunday evening, October 16, 1859, Brown gave his final orders, directing his men not to take a life where they could avoid it. Placing a few pikes and other implements in his one-horse wagon, he started with his company of eighteen followers at eight o'clock, leaving five men behind. They cut the telegraph wires on the way, and reached Harper's Ferry about eleven o'clock—fourteen white men and four Negroes with their leader. Brown himself broke open the gates of the United States armory, took the watchmen prisoners, and made that place his headquarters.

Separating his men into small detachments, he then took possession of and attempted to hold the two bridges, the arsenal, and the rifle factory. Next, Brown sent six of his followers five miles into the countryside to bring in several prominent slaveowners with their slaves. This was accomplished before daylight, and all were brought as prisoners to Brown, at the armory.

At dawn irregular street firing broke out between Brown's sentinels and citizens who had firearms. The alarm was carried to neighboring towns.

By Monday noon Brown was driven back to take refuge with his diminished force in the enginehouse, a low, strong brick building in the armory yard. They barricaded the windows, improvised loopholes, and took with them ten selected prisoners as hostages.

By this time the surrounding country had become thoroughly roused. Militia companies poured in from nearby towns to block any attempts by Brown and his little group to escape. By nightfall the government had sent to Harper's Ferry a detachment of United States marines under the command of Colonel Robert E. Lee.

At daylight on Tuesday, Brown was ordered to surrender. When he refused, a storming party of the marines battered in the door. One marine was shot dead in the assault. Brown fell under severe sword and bayonet wounds, two of his sons lay dead or dying, and four or five of his men were made prisoners. The great scheme of liberation, elaborately built up for nearly three years, was in utter collapse, after five minutes of conflict with Colonel Lee's troops, even though the would-be liberators had held the town for about thirty-six hours. The slaves from the surrounding plantations had failed to co-operate in the scheme.

Convicted of treason, John Brown was sentenced to be hanged on the second of December. His companions were to be executed on the sixteenth. From beginning to end this enterprise was illegal and rash, but it sprang from a generous and sincere impulse. The old man's courage and his utter devotion to the cause appealed strongly to the opponents of slavery. The seething conflict between bondage and liberty for the Negro was fast approaching a crisis, and the tragedy of Harper's Ferry may be considered an introductory act to the tremendous struggle that was to follow.

The unsuccessful raid and its leader's death by hanging was of the utmost importance in the development of events leading to the Civil War, as a violent climax to the political bitterness which had raged for several years. The destruction of the institution of slavery later became one of the underlying goals of the Civil War.

Had there been no John Brown we might never have had an Abraham Lincoln in the Presidency, for the debates with Douglas which brought him into national prominence in 1858 were mainly concerned with slavery. Without Lincoln as President, the Emancipation Proclamation which was to be issued just three years and one month after Brown's death might have been postponed many years.

Julia Ward Howe described the day of Brown's execution in Charlestown, Virginia, on December 2, 1859, as one of general mourning in New England. Shortly afterward, during the heat of the campaign for the Massachusetts governorship, a mass meeting honoring the Abolitionist candidate, John A. Andrew, was held in Boston's Faneuil Hall. That evening, crowds of young men and boys paraded the streets, singing to a familiar Mother Goose air the monotonous phrase:

> Tell John Andrew,
> Tell John Andrew,
> Tell John Andrew,
> John Brown's dead!

A little more than a year later the first shots against the flag of the United States at Fort Sumter stirred the nation into action and war became a reality. Almost immediately the Second Battalion of Massachusetts Infantry, nicknamed the Tigers, was assigned to occupy Fort Warren, one of the defenses of Boston Harbor, and place it in as good repair as possible.

Four men of the unit formed a quartet, and it was from this glee club that the entire company learned the Methodist hymn tune, originally composed by William Steffe in 1855. As a camp-meeting song, it had become popular with Negro churches and fire companies of Charleston, South Carolina:

> Say, brothers, will you meet us?
> Say, brothers, will you meet us?
> Say, brothers, will you meet us
> On Canaan's happy shore?

Steffe's tune was sung by a group of Negro girls at Shady Hole, Georgia, during Sherman's March to the Sea, when a Federal band struck up the well-known tune, and may therefore have been adapted by him from a Negro folk song.

In the six years between the song's composition and the outbreak of the war, the camp-meeting hymn had ample time to drift northward and become generally familiar, for it had already appeared in some of the contemporary Methodist hymnals. Thane Miller had a large part in its northern migration, for he is said to have introduced it at a convention of the Young Men's Christian Association at Albany, New York, some time in the latter part of 1859 or the early part of 1860.

James E. Greenleaf, an organist in a church in Charlestown, Massachusetts, near Boston, adapted the tune, and it was this amended form that made such a strong appeal to the soldiers. Patrick Gilmore, later to become the most famous bandmaster in the Union Army, played it for the men at Fort Warren regularly in his Saturday night concerts.

There was a majestic simplicity in the rhythm that helped to lighten labor; so while entrenchments were being thrown up by the soldiers and they were carrying away the rubbish of the old fort, the men sang the swinging tune with a vigor that made the picks and shovels resound to their task.

It was not long before a spirit of mischief prompted the young soldiers to improvise verses of a less sacred character and sing them to the old melody. As it happened, one of the singers in the Fort Warren quartet was an honest and simple Scottish sergeant named John Brown, who was the good-natured butt of their jokes. Finally, a jest was made of this similarity with the great Abolitionist. This is how the verses of the *John Brown Song,* as it came to be known, originated.

One evening when some of the men were returning to the fort in a rowboat, the query was shouted, "What's the news?", and promptly the retort came, "Why, John Brown's dead," leading to the first verse:

John Brown's body lies a-mouldering in the grave.

Referring to the frequent tours of guard duty and dress parades, someone added:

John Brown's knapsack is strapped upon his back.

Since the regimental chaplain was fond of calling the volunteers "the army of the Lord," the verse

He's gone to be a soldier in the army of the Lord

quite naturally followed.

The battalion, which became a part of the Twelfth Masschusetts Regiment, often called itself "Webster's cattle," after the name of its commander, Colonel Fletcher Webster, the son of the famous Daniel, hence the verse:

His pet lambs will meet him on the way.

The regiment was responsible for spreading the fame of the song beyond Fort Warren. The *John Brown Song* was readily adopted as its marching song. Many people heard it for the first time on Boston Common, where it was sung on July 18, 1861, when they received their colors from Edward Everett. The unit sang it as they marched down Broadway in New York City a week later en route to the Virginia battlefields. Baltimore heard it two days later.

In the latter part of 1861 the Boston firm of Oliver Ditson and Company published the song under the title of *Glory, Hallelujah!*

On March 1, 1862, at Charlestown, Virginia, on the spot where John Brown was hanged, the Webster regiment formally sang *John Brown's Body* in his memory. By that time the tune was taken up by the nation, and hundreds of soldiers were marching into battle with the name of John Brown on their lips.

The mention of the name of this martyr to the cause of Abolition was a particularly bitter taunt to Southerners. As the war progressed and the abolition of slavery became one of the principal objectives of continued struggle, Confederate President Jefferson Davis became a hated symbol, calling for an added verse:

They will hang Jeff Davis to a sour apple tree.

Later, as Union soldiers trudged many a long and weary mile, they sang with patriotic flourish a final added verse:

Now, three rousing cheers for the Union
    As we are marching on!

As in the case of *Dixie,* attempts to provide intelligent words in good grammatical form to replace the foolish stanzas resulted in failure. Edna Dean Proctor's version seemed ill-fitted to the tune:

John Brown died on a scaffold for the slave,
Dark was the hour when we dug his hallowed grave;
Now God avenges the life he gladly gave,
    Freedom reigns today!

CHORUS

John Brown's body lies a-mouldering in the grave;
John Brown lives in the triumphs of the brave;
John Brown's soul not a higher joy can crave—
    Freedom reigns today!

This poem, entitled *The President's Proclamation*, was issued immediately after Lincoln had freed the slaves.

One of the reasons for the song's wide use and extensive popularity was the simplicity of the rhyme, which so admirably matched the tune. Along with *Dixie*, *John Brown's Body* forms ample proof that stirring music does not necessarily require elegant verse in order to survive.

Only Julia Ward Howe was able to produce verses of dignity to the old tune. Even after her *Battle Hymn of the Republic* attained renown, the soldiers would not give up their beloved words.

With no attention to its original meaning, but for its sheer nonsense and rousing meter, *John Brown's Body* has been a favorite with American soldiers of two later wars, and, strangely enough, has been adopted by British soldiers, who are not at all bothered by its purely American sentiments.

John Brown's Body has been aptly characterized as "a song which sang itself into being of its own accord."

☆☆☆☆☆☆☆☆☆

The Battle Hymn
of the Republic

The Battle Hymn
of the Republic

Mine eyes have seen the glory of the coming of the
Lord:
He is trampling out the vintage where the grapes of
wrath are stored;
He hath loosed the fateful lightning of His terrible
swift sword;
His truth is marching on.

CHORUS
Glory, glory, hallelujah!
Glory, glory, hallelujah!
Glory, glory, hallelujah!
His truth is marching on.

I have seen Him in the watch-fires of a hundred cir-
cling camps,
They have builded Him an altar in the evening dews
and damps;
I have read His righteous sentence by the dim and
flaring lamps;
His day is marching on.

I have read His fiery gospel writ in rows of burnished
    steel!
"As ye deal with My contemners, so with you My
    grace shall deal!
Let the Hero, born of woman, crush the serpent with
    His heel,"
        Since God is marching on.

He has sounded forth the trumpet that shall never
    call retreat;
He is searching out the hearts of men before His judg-
    ment seat,
O be swift, my soul, to answer Him! be jubilant, my
    feet!
        Our God is marching on.

In the beauty of the lilies Christ was born across the
    sea,
With a glory in His bosom that transfigures you and
    me;
As He died to make men holy, let us die to make men
    free,
        While God is marching on.

JULIA WARD HOWE

1861

CHAPTER 13

The Battle Hymn
of the Republic

"The mightiest of our war songs is *John Brown's Body* ennobled into *The Battle Hymn of the Republic*," asserts a well-known writer on music. This one battle hymn seems to stand in a class of its own.

To have written such a deeply moving poem is glory and greatness enough for anyone, but, aside from this accomplishment, Julia Ward Howe was one of the most notable and gifted women our country has ever produced. When Brown University conferred upon her the honorary degree of Doctor of Letters, toward the end of her long, active, and productive life, she was formally characterized in the citation as "author, philanthropist, mother, friend of the slave, the prisoner, and of all who suffer, singer of the Battle Hymn of freedom."

This remarkable woman was born into a distinguished and wealthy New York banking family on May 27, 1819. Her childhood was marked by every advantage that wealth, culture, and social position could provide. A literary prodigy, at an early age she mastered several foreign languages which were to serve her well when she became an international figure and was sought out by the most prominent leaders of the day in every field of activity. Her interests were vast, and she found outlets for her energy in the sponsorship of many causes.

Throughout her busy life her primary ambition was to attain renown as a writer. Poems, dramas, and works on social problems flowed from her facile pen. But all her other literary productions are relatively insignificant in comparison with her major achievement, the writing of *The Battle Hymn of the Republic*. The tune, of course, was in existence long before the words were penned. The poem was written to fit the melody, and sprang into being as the inspiration of a single hour.

Miss Ward's social position permitted her to meet and become friendly with prominent persons of all types and in all professions. Her keen and universal interests caused her to absorb the knowledge and enthusiasm of everyone she met. Her inborn drive to solve challenging problems led her to become active later in many social movements —anti-slavery, woman's suffrage, advances in the status of women, and education. She was a doer as well as a thinker, and was content only when she was working to correct what she considered an evil condition in society. In these activities she was a liberal at a time when women were not expected to express themselves, and when taking a stand on the social questions of the day required great moral courage.

While visiting Charles Sumner and Henry Wadsworth Longfellow in Boston, as a young girl of twenty-two, Miss Ward was introduced by them to Dr. Samuel Gridley Howe, a man twenty years her senior. Dr. Howe so captivated the young woman by his many interests and accomplishments that she married him less than a year later, in April, 1843. An ardent believer in freedom, he had been so inspired by the spirit and example of Lord Byron that he had spent several years of his young manhood aiding the Greeks in their struggle for liberty against the Turks. At the time of his marriage he was head of the Perkins Institution for the Blind and had attained national celebrity as the instructor of Laura Bridgman, the first blind and deaf mute to learn and use the English language. He was active as a pioneer in promoting legislation for the sightless.

Mrs. Howe was given the opportunity of writing extensively when, in 1851, her husband became editor of the *Commonwealth,* a liberal journal, and encouraged her to fill its columns with articles on social and literary topics. Her writings, particularly on slavery, made the paper one of the most famous during the years when Abolition sentiment was gaining impetus in the Northern states.

When the Civil War broke out, Dr. Howe was beyond the age for military service, but he was still a lover of freedom and a devoted enemy of slavery. As a skilled physician, he was fitted to render invaluable assistance to the Union cause, and he became an officer in the United States Sanitary Commission, the forerunner of the American Red Cross. His main activity was the investigation of the condition and health of soldiers in the Union Army.

The capital city was naturally the great center of interest at the time. In December, 1861, Dr. and Mrs. Howe, accompanied by the Reverend James Freeman Clarke, a Unitarian clergyman of Boston, Mrs. Clarke and Governor John A. Andrew of Massachusetts, visited Washington for a few days. The defeat at Bull Run had removed all hope of a short war and an easy Union victory, and had sobered those who had thought it what the New York *Times* called "an unborn tadpole." War, terrible and realistic, was in everyone's thoughts. Mrs. Howe became conscious of its deadly import during the railroad trip to the capital, when she saw in the darkness the small fires of the pickets on guard along the route.

Since the beginning of the conflict, Mrs. Howe had strongly felt her ineffectiveness to make a contribution to the Union cause. Her own words written many years later in her autobiography expressed this feeling. "I distinctly remember that a feeling of discouragement came over me as I drew near to the city of Washington," she said. "I thought of the women of my acquaintance whose sons or husbands were fighting our great battle, the women themselves serving in the hospitals or busying themselves with the work of the Sanitary Commission. . . . I could not leave my nursery to follow the march of our armies, neither had I the practical deftness which the preparing and packing of sanitary stores demanded. Something seemed to say to me, 'You would be glad to serve, but you cannot help anyone; you have nothing to give, and there is nothing for you to do.' Yet because of my sincere desire, a word was given me to say, which did strengthen the hearts of those who fought in the field and those who languished in prison."

A journey among the soldiers gave her this opportunity. The Union Army of the Potomac, of which McClellan had become commander in November, was encamped several miles from the city across the Potomac River in Virginia, and one day the Boston visitors drove out from Washington to witness a review of the troops. Dr. Howe also wished to inspect the conditions under which the soldiers lived. While they were watching the maneuvers, a sudden attack was made by the enemy. So, instead of the promised parade, the group heard scattered gunfire and watched a detachment of reinforcements race to the aid of a small force of Union soldiers which had been surprised and surrounded.

The regiments on the parade ground were dismissed and ordered to march back to their individual camps. These troops filled the roads and delayed the progress of the Howe carriage on its homeward journey.

Mrs. Howe had a well-trained, clear voice. As the progress toward the city was very slow due to the sea of soldiers on the road, she began to sing patriotic and army songs in which the rest of the party joined. *John Brown's Body* seemed especially to please the marching men, who took up the strain, calling out from time to time, "Good for you! Give us some more!"

The flippancy of the words seemed out of place in the martial atmosphere, and Dr. Clarke turned to Mrs. Howe and said, "Why don't you write some good words for that stirring tune, words worthy of it, and worthy of our soldiers?" She replied that she had often wished to do just that, but had not as yet found anything in her mind leading toward it. She was, she told the clergyman, unequal to the task, but he insisted that she could do it. "And so," she later admitted, "to pacify the dear old man, I promised to try."

Either that promise or the swinging tune sung by the marching soldiers made such a deep impression on Mrs. Howe's mind that, when she awakened before dawn the next morning in her room at Willard's Hotel, she found herself attempting to give form and shape to shadowy words that might possibly be sung to the *John Brown's Body* music. She has described how line after line swiftly molded itself in her brain.

When she had thought out the last of the five stanzas, she said to herself, "I must get up and write these verses down, lest I fall asleep again and forget them."

She therefore sprang hastily out of bed and groped around in the dim gray light until she found a pen and a scrap of Sanitary Commission paper. "I scrawled the verses almost without looking at the paper. I had learned to do this when attacks of versification had previously come upon me in the night and I feared to have a light lest I should wake the baby, who slept near me. . . . Having completed the writing, I returned to bed and fell asleep, saying to myself, 'I like this better than most things I have written.' "

When Mrs. Howe showed the poem to Dr. Clarke a day or two later he was greatly pleased, saying, "I told you I knew you could do it." After her return to Boston she took the verses to James T. Fields, then editor of the *Atlantic Monthly*. He seemed pleased with the lyric beauty and the spirit of the poem, and accepted it for publication, paying her five dollars for it. Under the title *The Battle Hymn of the Republic,* suggested by Mr. Fields, the poem appeared on the first page of the February, 1862, issue of the magazine, strangely without the name of the author.

Mrs. Howe later wrote that, though they were praised by some, the verses received no special attention at first. She did not realize how rapidly the hymn was making its way and how strong a hold it was quietly taking upon people everywhere. In the course of the year 1862, the poem was widely reprinted, with her name finally identified as the author, in newspapers and army hymnbooks and in many sheet-music editions. It became, in fact, the poem of the hour, and before long the great Union armies were marching to its stanzas, which had finally replaced the words of *John Brown's Body* and given dignity to the well-known tune.

Julia Ward Howe was not content to rest on the well-deserved fame which *The Battle Hymn of the Republic* brought her. In the after-war years of her long life she threw herself into a multitude of activities which were to make her one of the truly great and productive American women of her day. Following her husband's death in 1876, she spent much time lecturing and traveling. As a sincere and effective speaker she was in demand everywhere in connection with her work as feminist and social reformer.

She was ordained as a Unitarian minister and became president of the newly formed Association for the Advancement of Women.

Wherever she spoke, *The Battle Hymn of the Republic* was sung either before or after her lecture. Her interest in the welfare of Negroes was intensified after slavery was abolished. She was a militant pioneer in the woman's suffrage movement. Some of her greatest achievements were accomplished during the decade after her eightieth birthday. At ninety she was still active and tireless. The next year she received the degree of Doctor of Letters from Smith College, appearing at the exercises in a wheel chair.

In her old age she became a kind of American institution, a lady of first rank. People came to Boston on pilgrimages to see her, as they might an historical monument. Audiences rose in respect when she entered a theater. The gentle face, framed by a lace kerchief over her hair, became familiar to millions who were not even born until after the Civil War.

Few American women have lived so long and distinguished a life, and few have possessed in such a remarkable degree the gentle art of growing old gracefully. When she was nearing the end of her life she confided to a friend that the world grew constantly more interesting to her. "The bowl of life," she said, "grows sweeter as I drink it; all the sugar is at the bottom." The end came on October 17, 1910, in her ninety-first year.

The Battle Hymn of the Republic made a great contribution to the Union war effort. Mrs. Howe's composition proved to be exactly the type of song needed at the time, and its popularity increased as the war continued on its weary course. President Lincoln never tired of hearing the song, and each time he wept unashamedly. Her words touched the hearts of soldiers and civilians alike, for they possessed a grandeur and loftiness found in few other Civil War songs.

She it was who produced the most moving verses of the war and gave to the care-pressed people a song of true dignity and religious feeling, something which most of the twelve hundred compositions submitted in the national song contest held in mid-1861 failed to express.

Some of the telling and vivid phrases used in the poem are, to quote a critic, "almost unmatched in their combination of words and images, and form a rare example of the kind of inspiration and intensity of feeling which produces a truly superior piece of poetry." In few works will one find such graphic phrases as "the grapes of wrath," "the fateful lightning of His terrible swift sword," "His fiery gospel writ in rows of burnished steel," "the trumpet that shall never call retreat," and "a glory in His bosom that transfigures you and me."

Speaking about her masterpiece after the war, Julia Ward Howe had this to say: "The wild echoes of that fearful struggle have long since died away, and with them all memories of unkindness between ourselves and our Southern brethren. But those who once loved my hymn still sing it. I hope and believe that it stands for what our whole country now believes in—that is, the sacredness of human liberty. My poem did some service in the Civil

War. I wish very much that it may do good service in the Peace, which I pray God may never more be broken."

One characterization of *The Battle Hymn of the Republic* appears fittingly to summarize the power of this matchless song: "This soul-inspiring poem was the incarnation of patriotism and martial feeling. It was struck out of the white heat of unconscious inspiration, the soul's product of a mighty moment. It is the most resonant and elevating of all America's battle hymns."

☆☆☆☆☆☆☆☆☆☆

Marching
Through Georgia

Marching Through Georgia

Bring the good old bugle, boys! we'll sing another
    song—
Sing it with a spirit that will start the world along—
Sing it as we used to sing it, fifty thousand strong,
    While we were marching through Georgia.

CHORUS

    Hurrah! hurrah! we bring the jubilee!
    Hurrah! hurrah! the flag that makes you free!
    So we sang the chorus from Atlanta to the sea,
    While we were marching through Georgia.

How the darkies shouted when they heard the joyful
    sound!
How the turkeys gobbled which our commissary
    found!
How the sweet potatoes even started from the ground,
    While we were marching through Georgia.

Yes, and there were Union men who wept with joyful
    tears,
When they saw the honored flag they had not seen for
    years;

Hardly could they be restrained from breaking forth
    in cheers,
  While we were marching through Georgia.

"Sherman's dashing Yankee boys will never reach the
    coast!"
So the saucy rebels said, and 'twas a handsome boast.
Had they not forgot, alas, to reckon with the host,
  While we were marching through Georgia.

So we made a thoroughfare for Freedom and her
    train,
Sixty miles in latitude—three hundred in the main;
Treason fled before us, for resistance was in vain,
  While we were marching through Georgia.

                              HENRY CLAY WORK
1865

CHAPTER 14

Marching Through Georgia

With the exception of *The Star-Spangled Banner,* few of our most popular national songs have a single incident as their subject. This is undoubtedly because, as an event loses its contemporary significance, this type of song rarely retains its appeal. This fact explains why "topical" song writers seldom achieve lasting fame.

The songs of Henry Clay Work, however, are an exception, for his compositions about the slave are still appealing. Furthermore, *Marching Through Georgia,* dealing with Sherman's March to the Sea, is undoubtedly known and sung today with as much fervor as it was in the last days of the Civil War.

Few American tunes have been as popular in foreign armies, with or without the 1865 words. The Russian band entering Harbin during the Russo-Japanese War in 1903 played the tune. Many a British regiment left England for France during World War I to its stirring strains. Its rhythms marked the cadence when American troops marched into Tunis in World War II. For many years after the Civil War, every encampment or parade of the Grand Army of the Republic featured the song.

Sherman heard it so often that he developed an intense dislike for it, because it had become closely associated with an exploit which, if it could not be forgotten, he wished to be considered only as one of his many campaigns. He felt that it directed attention from other and what he believed to be far greater strategic movements, and from the successful fighting in the final months of the war.

The tune pursued him after the war from city to city, and even to foreign lands. At the 1890 G.A.R. convention in Boston, the old veteran, its guest of honor, stood for seven hours in the reviewing stand while he listened to *Marching Through Georgia* rising from 250 bands and one hundred fife and drum corps! "If I had thought," he once said, "when I made that march that it would have inspired anyone to compose a piece, I would have marched around the state!"

Southerners, especially Georgians, even today dislike and resent the song intensely, for it recalls the most tragic and destructive single episode in the War Between the States, a carnival of ruin difficult to forgive and certainly impossible to forget. Because it was so often sung by Northerners gloating over the effects of the march, the composition was the most resented of all the songs of the Civil War, and was called "a hymn of hate."

But, apart from its subject, *Marching Through Georgia* has no equal among Civil War marching songs, putting quickness into laggard feet and giving a lift to weary soldiers. One critic has said, *"Marching Through Georgia will be marching on long after the majority of our contemporary best-sellers will have been buried without taps."*

The song was written early in 1865 by Henry Clay Work, who was born October 1, 1832, at Middletown, Connecticut. He was therefore still a young man when the war inspired him to musical composition. George F. Root was his sole rival as the most popular Northern composer, and all his songs were published by the firm of Root and Cady.

Mr. Work had little musical education, yet he had a feeling for events and movements, and taught himself simple harmony. A printer by trade, he often composed the words of a song while he set up type. Later, when he had access to music type at Root's Chicago establishment, he would compose in his mind, and set up the music directly into type without writing down the words and notes on paper. These pieces seldom required more than two or three simple alterations. *Marching Through Georgia* is in this way probably unique among the war songs of the world, for it was composed "free hand" without appearing in manuscript.

In Connecticut Work's father had been persecuted as an active and outspoken Abolitionist, leading the family to move to Illinois. There he was imprisoned for maintaining a station on the underground railway, which enabled fugitive slaves to escape into Canada. These personal experiences gave the young printer a keen sympathy with the Southern Negro. As slavery began to become a recognized basis of the war, Work eagerly followed Lincoln's actions in anticipation of the Emancipation Proclamation.

Accordingly, most of his other well-known songs deal with this subject.

Kingdom Coming (1862) was Work's first song of the Negro. In his autobiography, Root describes how his association with the would-be composer began.

"One day early in the war a quiet and rather solemn-looking young man, poorly clad, was sent up to my room from the store with a song for me to examine. I looked at it and then at him in astonishment. It was *Kingdom Coming*—full of bright good sense and comical situations in its darkey dialect, the words fitting the melody almost as aptly and neatly as Gilbert fits Sullivan,—the melody decidedly good and taking, and the whole exactly suited to the times. 'Did you write this, words and music?' I asked. A gentle 'yes' was the answer. 'What is your business, if I may enquire?' 'I am a printer.' 'Would you rather write music than set type?' 'Yes.' 'Well, if this is a specimen of what you can do, I think you may give up the printing business.' He liked the idea very much, and an arrangement was soon made. He needed some musical help that I could give him, and we needed just such songs as he could write. The connection, which continued some years, proved very profitable both to him and to us."

Kingdom Coming is very similar to Stephen Foster's *De Camptown Races,* and is often confused with it. The song makes no reference to Negro freedom; its jovial dialect verses merely picture a Southern plantation owner fleeing before the advance of the Union Army:

> Say, darkies, hab you seen de massa
> Wid de mufftas on his face,

Go 'long de road sometime dis mornin'
Like he gwine to leab de place?
He seen a smoke way up de ribber
Where de Linkum gumboats lay;
He took his hat and lef' berry sudden
An' I 'spec he's run away!

CHORUS

De massas run, ha! ha!
De darkies stay, ho! ho!
It mus' be now de kingdom comin'
An' de year of Jubilo.

The year of Jubilo (jubilee) was the long-anticipated time when the slaves were to gain their freedom.

This song was rivaled by its sequel, *Babylon Is Fallen*, published in mid-1863, when the liberated colored men began to join the Union Army as laborers and soldiers:

Don't you see de black clouds
Risin' ober yonder
Where de massa's ole plantation am?
Nebber you be frightened,
Dem is only darkies
Come to jine and fight for Uncle Sam.

CHORUS

Look out, dar, now, we's a-gwine to shoot!
Look out, dar, don't you understand?
Babylon is fallen! Babylon is fallen!
And we's a-gwine to occupy de land.

In the second verse a Negro regiment makes a prisoner of the massa, a Confederate colonel.

Work's third important Negro song was *Wake, Nicodemus,* which tells of an old slave buried in the trunk of a hollow tree. He had requested that he be awakened at the first breaking of the Day of Jubilo, which had been made possible when the Emancipation Proclamation came into effect.

All the songs of this composer are characterized by a lightness and joyfulness which had a tremendous current appeal amid the sorrows and burdens of wartime.

His first song, *Grafted Into the Army,* had had as its subject an illiterate Irish mother who bewailed the fact that her young son Jimmy had been drafted (grafted) and forced to join the Union Army:

> O Jimmy, farewell! Your brothers fell
> Way down in Alabamy;
> I thought they would spare a lone widder's heir,
> But they grafted him into the army.

But it was Sherman's March to the Sea which inspired Henry Clay Work to produce his masterpiece, *Marching Through Georgia.*

The history of warfare has few campaigns with such appalling destruction as that spread by Sherman's troops. The march, during November and December, 1864, was the final blow from which the Confederacy was never to recover. Leaving Atlanta, sixty thousand troops moved in several lines, cutting a swath sixty miles wide across

Georgia, leaving complete ruin in its wake. Pillaging and foraging by "bummers" reduced the area to utter desolation. The song describes various aspects of the march.

The seven thousand "joyful darkies" who joined the rear guard of the army before it reached Savannah, and the abundant food supplies foraged from the countryside form the subject of the second verse. Next, Work cites, as George F. Root did in *Tramp, Tramp, Tramp* and *On, On, On* the liberation of the Union Army prisoners along the route. Finally, he praises the whole achievement. *Marching Through Georgia* is full of joy and mirth, one of the reasons for its permanence.

The campaign took its popular name "Sherman's March to the Sea" from the song of that title which the general preferred. This was written by an officer of an Iowa regiment, Lieutenant Samuel H. M. Byers, who was liberated from the Confederate prison at Columbia, South Carolina, when Sherman's forces occupied the city. Byers became an aide to and a favorite of the commander whom he had honored in the song. It sold over a million copies, though overshadowed by Work's more joyful composition.

Henry Clay Work continued his writing after the war, and even after Root's business had been destroyed in the Chicago fire. *Grandfather's Clock,* with its tick-tock rhythm, was immensely appealing. His *Come Home, Father,* picturing a little girl begging her father to leave a saloon, became one of the most famous of all temperance songs. Though he had made a fortune from his over two hundred songs, Work invested unwisely and lost most of it. He died in Connecticut in 1884, at the age of fifty-two.

The captivating rhythm of *Marching Through Georgia* survives today as an unsurpassed light marching song. The chorus of few American songs rings out with quite so joyous a swell as when voices join in the refrain

While we were marching through Georgia.

☆☆☆☆☆☆☆☆☆

Other Civil War Songs

CHAPTER 15

Other Civil War Songs

The tragic conflict between North and South which threatened to split the United States in the early 1860s was unique among our wars in that music played a large part in it. Several thousand songs were published during the four years of what has aptly been termed the Singing Sixties. These compositions honored the military and political leaders; celebrated victories and bemoaned defeats; pictured the soldier in camp, on the march and in battle; and told of the joys and sorrows of the families on the home front.

A few of these songs, already discussed in previous chapters, have become a part of our musical heritage and have outlived the particular circumstances in which they were written. A half-dozen others deserve to be called national songs because, though not as frequently sung or as well known today, they were a vital part of the conflict which was the most personal of our wars, in one way or another affecting every person then living in the United States.

Seldom has any war affected so many of the home folks. The war years were sad for them. Mothers, sisters, and sweethearts lived in dread of receiving news that their soldier boys were killed, wounded, or taken prisoner. The enforced separation of sweethearts was the subject of many mournful ballads. The most-sung of these, *Weeping, Sad and Lonely, or When This Cruel War Is Over,* written by Charles Carroll Sawyer, sold over a million copies, a tremendous sale a century ago, and enjoyed equal popularity in North and South:

> Weeping, sad and lonely;
> Hopes and fears how vain!
> When this cruel war is over,
> Praying that we meet again!

A song written by a Northerner, J. P. Webster, before the war, was the most popular of the love songs, attaining wide popularity in the Confederacy. *Lorena* told of unrequited love, and no Civil War novel with a Southern background is complete today without a scene where the beautiful heroine, accompanying herself on the piano, sings this song.

Union rallying songs were heard everywhere during the early war years. As volunteers, the boys in blue answered the call to the colors to *The Battle-Cry of Freedom* and many another song. As the war progressed President Lincoln found it necessary to increase the calls and his quotas to fill the ranks.

The 1862 call for 300,000 volunteers came at a time of Union discouragement, when the army seemed unable to take decisive action in advancing toward the main goal, the capture of Richmond, the Confederate capital. A northern Abolitionist Quaker, James Sloan Gibbons, at that time wrote one of the most stirring of all calls to arms and called it *We Are Coming, Father Abraham:*

We are coming, Father Abraham, three hundred thousand
more,
From Mississippi's winding stream and from New England's shore;
We leave our ploughs and workshops, our wives and children dear,
With hearts too full for utterance, with but a silent tear;
We dare not look behind us, but steadfastly before.
We are coming, Father Abraham, three hundred thousand
more!

If you look across the hilltops that meet the northern sky,
Long moving lines of rising dust your vision may descry;
And now the wind an instant tears the cloudy veil aside,
And floats aloft our spangled flag, in glory and in pride;
And bayonets in the sunlight gleam, and bands brave music pour.
We are coming, Father Abraham, three hundred thousand
more!

The soldier was not forgotten in songs expressing a depth of personal feeling. *Tenting on the Old Camp Ground* appealed particularly to them, not as an exciting battle song, but as a description of what they were thinking. Its author was Walter C. Kittredge of New Hampshire. He had been drafted in the Union army in the early months of 1863, and expected soon to leave for the front. He had been a professional singer, so it was natural that, thinking of the coming separation from his wife and daughter, he composed a song expressing his emotion.

The words appealed to soldiers and civilians alike. The chorus aptly expressed the heavy-heartedness of a war-weary people, and the verses seemed written expressly for the soldier far from home and facing an unknown and uncertain future:

We're tenting tonight on the old camp ground, give us a
    song to cheer
Our weary hearts, a song of home and friends we love so
    dear.

CHORUS

Many are the hearts that are weary tonight, wishing
    for the war to cease;
Many are the hearts that are looking for the right, to
    see the dawn of peace.
Tenting tonight, tenting tonight, tenting on the old
    camp ground.

We've been tenting tonight on the old camp ground,
    thinking of days gone by,
Of the loved ones at home that gave us the hand, and the
    tear that said "Goodbye!"

We are tired of war on the old camp ground, many are
    dead and gone,
Of the brave and true who've left their homes, others been
    wounded long.

We've been fighting today on the old camp ground, many
    are lying near;
Some are dead, and some are dying, many are in tears.

        (Final lines of last chorus):
        Dying tonight, dying tonight,
        Dying on the old camp ground.

But Kittredge did not serve on the battlefield after all.
He was rejected for military service on medical grounds.
So he joined the famed Hutchinson family of singers and
toured with them for twenty years thereafter.

The touching and plaintive words of *Tenting Tonight,*
as it was popularly known, so perfectly matched to the
music, were favorites of both soldiers and civilians. No
program of war songs was complete without a quartet
rendition of the song, with the echoing strains of the
chorus tugging at the heartstrings of the audience. Every
local reunion and meeting of the Grand Army of the
Republic and all its national conventions, or encamp-
ments as they were called, featured the song, which might
appropriately be termed one of the most affecting of the
Civil War period.

One of the most appealing among the hundreds of songs
concerning the life of the soldier in the army was *All Quiet*

Along the Potomac. During the long periods between major battles and campaigns, a soldier's main assignment was the lonely one of picket and sentry duty. The song was based on an actual incident claimed as having taken place during the time of inactivity following the first Battle of Bull Run, while the forces of both sides were gathering strength. For many days the newspapers could merely report in their headlines "All Quiet Along the Potomac," for there were no major battles to describe, and the people were in a tense period of expectation of great events in the future.

According to the story, a Confederate soldier, said to be Lamar Fontaine of the Second Virginia Cavalry, was standing night guard on a lonely outpost with one of his best friends, John Moore. After completing his six-hour assignment, he awakened his sleeping friend to take over. Moore stirred the glowing coals of the fire. The flames which leaped up revealed the position to the enemy pickets stationed on the opposite bank of the Potomac River, and made him a perfect target, framed in the fire's light. The bullet of a Union sharpshooter found its mark in Moore.

As he determined that his friend had been killed, Fontaine's eyes fell upon the headlines of a newspaper lying on the ground: "All Quiet Along the Potomac." The next day he wrote the poem:

"All quiet along the Potomac," they say,
   Except now and then a stray picket
Is shot, as he walks on his beat, to and fro,
   By a rifleman hid in the thicket. . . .

All quiet along the Potomac tonight,
　No sound save the rush of the river;
While soft falls the dew on the face of the dead—
　The picket's off duty forever.

The full poem has five stanzas.

So popular was the work, set to music by both Northern and Southern composers, that the commanders of the opposing forces, the Union Army of the Potomac and the Confederate Army of Northern Virginia, issued a joint order prohibiting the barbarous custom of picket fire, again exhibiting the powerful influence which a song can exert in times of war.

No discussion of Civil War songs can be considered complete without the one and only *When Johnny Comes Marching Home*. Written in 1863, its rousing strains served to foretell the happy day when the war would be over.

The Louis Lambert whose name was on the title page was actually Patrick S. Gilmore, the most famous of Union bandmasters. He it was who had introduced *John Brown's Body* to the troops at Fort Warren in Boston Harbor in 1861. In 1863 he was in charge of all the military bands in the New Orleans district, and composed *When Johnny Comes Marching Home* for a mammoth concert, at a time when the end of the war seemed to be approaching, a hope which proved to be vain. The lyric was adapted from an Irish folksong:

When Johnny comes marching home again, Hurrah! Hurrah!

We'll give him a hearty welcome then, Hurrah! Hurrah!
The men will cheer, the boys will shout,
The ladies they will all turn out,

CHORUS

And we'll all feel gay when Johnny comes marching home.

The old church-bell will peal with joy, Hurrah! Hurrah!
To welcome home our darling boy, Hurrah! Hurrah!
The village lads and lassies say,
With roses they will strew the way,

Let love and friendship on that day, Hurrah! Hurrah!
Their choicest treasures then display, Hurrah! Hurrah!
And let each one perform some part
To fill with joy the warrior's heart.

Not even the shock of the people in both North and South
when the war's end was long delayed could lessen the effect
of the song in the lift of spirits it gave them momentarily.
And its uplifting effect did not end with the Civil War.
The soldiers of all the three later wars have marched
gaily home to this unexcelled tune.

The story of the Civil War can be completely told in
the words of the songs which were sung alike by the people
and the soldiers. The effect of music in the armies and on
the home front is recounted in scores of contemporary
memoirs, all attesting to the power of songs in every sort
of situation. One story told by a Union naval officer may
serve to show the powerful influence exerted by music.

"A day or two after General Lee's surrender in April,
1865," he wrote, "I left our ship for a run up to occupied

Richmond, where I was joined by the ship's surgeon, the paymaster and one of the junior officers. Dinner being over, the doctor, who was a fine player, opened the piano, saying, 'Boys, we've got our old quartet here; let's have a sing!' As the house opposite was occupied by paroled Confederate officers, no patriotic songs were sung. Soon the lady of the house handed me this note: 'Compliments of General —— and staff. Will the gentlemen kindly allow us to come over and hear them sing?'

"Of course we consented and presently they came. Introductions and the usual interchange of civilities over, we sang glees and college songs for them, until at last the General said, 'Excuse me, gentlemen, you sing delightfully, but what *we* want to hear is your army songs.'

"Then we gave them the army songs with spirit—*Battle Hymn of the Republic, John Brown's Body, We Are Coming, Father Abraham, Tenting on the Old Camp Ground,* through the whole catalogue, up to *The Star-Spangled Banner,* to which many a Confederate foot beat time, as if it had never stepped to any but the music of the Union.

"When the applause had subsided at the close of our concert, a tall, fine-looking fellow in a major's uniform, exclaimed, 'Gentlemen, if we'd had your songs, we'd have licked you out of your boots! Who couldn't have marched or fought with such songs as these?'

"This little company of Union singers and Confederate listeners, after a pleasant and interesting interchange of stories of army experiences, then separated. As the General shook hands at parting, he said to me, 'Well, the time may come when we can all sing *The Star-Spangled Banner* again!'

"And we of a second generation," he concluded, "have witnessed this patriotic wish come true."

☆☆☆☆☆☆☆☆☆☆

The Songs
of the Negro

CHAPTER 16

The Songs of the Negro

The story is told of a music teacher who asked a young girl pupil to define a folk song. "A folk song," she announced immediately, "is one written by nobody." Folk music springs from the people. Such songs are not created through the combined inspiration of a poet and a composer; like Topsy, they "just grow."

The true folk music of the United States is that of the American Negro. Many feel that the American Indians, the true natives of our country, might have furnished our folk music had they not been overrun and practically exterminated by the white man. Instead, it fell to the lot of the Negro, imported from Africa, first as slaves, then as free men, to contribute our true native music. This part of our musical heritage and culture extends from the days of the early plantations, with the religious songs and spirituals, through the time of minstrelsy, and more recently in the twentieth century through the development of ragtime, jazz, and the "blues."

Folk music is anonymous. No one can identify the names of the authors of the words or the composers of the music. Such songs may exist for generations without being written down, and they are kept alive in what is called an oral tradition. They are sung and re-sung, often with changes, as they are handed down from generation to generation. The folk music of the Negro did not even become a subject of study and attention until after the Civil War, when the newly freed colored man became recognized as a substantial minority group in our country. The first book of Negro songs was published in 1867, and included spirituals of the colored men at Port Royal, South Carolina, which had been written down by members of an educational mission sent there by Northerners seeking to improve the conditions of their life.

Before the war, of course, the music of the Negro was known and accepted in the Southern slave states as a part of the plantation life. The earliest tunes which have finally been recorded and become a part of our heritage are in the main religious—the spirituals and "sorrow" songs. These are the emotional outbursts and creation of simple people who have a natural feeling for music and a gift for music-making. The spirituals expressed the true feelings of a people in bondage who must endure a hard life before the long-hoped-for day of liberation and freedom will arrive.

The editors of the first published songbook noted that "their wild, sad strains tell, as the sufferers themselves could, of crushed hopes, keen sorrow and a dull daily misery which covered them as hopelessly as the fog from the rice swamps. . . . The words breathe a trusting faith for rest in the future."

Booker T. Washington once wrote of his people's songs: "No race has ever sung so sweetly or with such perfect charity, while looking forward to the year of Jubilee. . . . The spirituals breathe a childlike faith in a personal Father, and glow with the hope that the children of bondage will eventually pass out of the wilderness of slavery into the land of freedom."

The plantation songs known as spirituals were spontaneous outbursts of intense religious fervor, and had their origin chiefly in camp meetings, revivals, and religious gatherings. Groups of slaves would gather together for prayer and singing. The words of the elders would find response in the "shouts" of the audience as their excitement increased. Finally, a voice would begin a song, making up the words to express the feelings of the moment. Constant repetition made the song familiar.

When Colonel Thomas W. Higginson was in command of one of the first regiments of Negro troops in the Union Army he became fascinated by the natural love of music of his singing men. When he asked an oarsman how the spirituals originated, he received the reply, "Some good sperichels are start jess out o' curiosity. I been a-raise to sing, myself, once," that is, he was a natural singer from birth. A South Carolina volunteer soldier answered the same question with, "Dey make 'em, sah. Dey work it in till dey get it right, and dat's de way." These definitions are as good an explanation of what constitutes true folk music as one can find.

The recognition of the contribution of the Negro to our

national music has been fairly recent. After the Civil War, in the 1870s, America became acquainted with the music of the Negro through the singers of the newly formed Southern colleges—Fisk University and Hampton and Tuskegee industrial schools—who made continuous country-wide tours giving fund-raising concerts.

Later Negro musicians and poets, among them Henry T. Burleigh and J. Rosamond Johnson and his brother James Weldon Johnson, collected and arranged the songs of their race. In more modern times such singers as Paul Robeson, Roland Hayes, and Marian Anderson have been major performers of Negro music.

No longer oddities, the Negro songs have become a recognized part of our American life, and a number of them are as well known as the more formal compositions of white composers. Through familiarity and repetition they have become truly national songs, not only because they are representative of our country's largest minority but because they are human, simple, and honest.

These songs are without date, composers, or locality, for they are our folk music. At least half a dozen are worthy of a place next to our exalted songs of sentiment and home and our hymns, and they are completely unique: *Steal Away, Swing Low, Sweet Chariot, Deep River, Nobody Knows de Trouble I've Seen, Roll, Jordan, Roll,* and *Go Down Moses.*

Steal Away, sung at secret meetings of slaves, represents the hope of the Negro for an eventual happiness:

> Steal away, steal away,
> Steal away to Jesus.

Steal away, steal away,
Steal away home,
I ain't got long to stay here,

while *Swing Low, Sweet Chariot* also expresses this hope of a future home better than his present lot of bondage to the white man:

Swing low, sweet chariot,
Comin' for to carry me home.

Religion, as exemplified in revivals and camp meetings, can prove a solace, says *Deep River:*

Deep river, my home is over Jordan,
Deep river, Lord, I want to cross over into camp-ground

where peace can be found in the promised land.

The burden of slavery called forth another hope for rest and comfort in religion, represented by a personalized Jesus, in *Nobody Knows de Trouble I See:*

Nobody knows de trouble I see,
Nobody knows but Jesus. . . . Glory, hallelujah!
Sometimes I'm up, sometimes I'm down, Oh, yes, Lord;
Sometimes I'm almos' to de groun', Oh, yes, Lord.

The liberation from bondage may only come with death, according to *Roll Jordan, Roll:*

Roll Jordan, roll, I wanter go to heav'n when I die,
To hear ol' Jordan roll.

Just as the children of Israel found release through the
leadership of Moses, says *Go Down Moses,* the Negroes
"oppressed so hard they could not stand," may eventually
be freed:

> Go down, Moses,
> 'Way down in Egypt land,
> Tell ole Pharaoh,
> To let my people go.

All these songs are extremely simple, and almost primi-
tive. The words lack the polish of the poet, yet their meaning is clear. Negro spirituals are characterized by a deep
and continuous undercurrent of sadness, the true reflection
of the condition of the race. These form true folk music
because they are unsophisticated, unpolished, and uncom
plicated.

The Negro has, of course, been pictured in many songs
by composers of the white race, notably Stephen Collins
Foster. Minstrel songs presented the opposite side of the
coin, the colored man's happiness and simple mirth and
gaiety. Few of the native Negro songs, however, reflect this
phase of his life, for the slave's lot was not basically happy.
Only in the more modern contributions to American ragtime and jazz can one glimpse evidences of the Negro's joy
in living.

At least one Negro composer deserves a place of honor
among the makers of our national songs. James Bland, born

in 1854 on Long Island of mixed Negro, Indian, and white parentage, has been called the Negro Stephen Foster. In fact, most people think his outstanding song, *Carry Me Back to Old Virginny*, was written by Foster.

When very young, Bland ran away to join a minstrel troupe as a banjoist and singer, and except for a short period attending Howard University, from which he was graduated in 1873, spent his entire life thereafter in the world of the theater, being somewhat unique in that, when minstrels were ordinarily white men with faces darkened by burnt cork, he was a true Negro. He lived many years in Europe and proved to be the most successful American minstrel there. Though he made a great deal of money from his profession, he died penniless and obscure in 1911, when fifty-seven years old.

During his lifetime James Bland wrote nearly seven hundred songs, two of which have earned him lasting fame. Both these compositions, *In the Evening By the Moonlight* and *Carry Me Back to Old Virginny*, were written when he visited a plantation on the James River, in the Tidewater section of Virginia near Williamsburg, where the life of the freed Negroes was happy. This was when he was a bare twenty years old, and the quiet, restful life made a deep impression on him. He saw the Negroes gather in front of their cabins in the mild summer night:

> In de ebening by de moonlight
>   You could hear us darkies singing;
> In de ebening by de moonlight
>   You could hear de banjos ringing;

How de old folks would enjoy it,
    They would sit all night and listen,
As we sang in de ebening by de moonlight.

Returning to this same plantation in 1878, Bland was again impressed by the calm peace of life in Virginia, and in *Carry Me Back to Old Virginny* he pictured the yearnings of an old Negro to return to his native state:

Carry me back to old Virginny,
There's where the cotton and the corn and 'tatoes grow,
There's where the birds warble sweet in the springtime,
There's where the old darkey's heart am long'd to go.
There's where I labored so hard for old Massa,
Day after day in the field of yellow corn.
No place on earth do I love more sincerely
Than old Virginny, the state where I was born.

The song's title was suggested by a girl friend of Bland's when he was attending Howard University in Washington, D.C. She had told him of a dream she had of being carried back to her home at this plantation. Bland merely transferred her thoughts to those of the old colored man.

Carry Me Back to Old Virginny was adopted as the official song of the state in 1940. Virginia Governor William A. Tuck commented on the song at a 1946 ceremony dedicating a tombstone, gift of the state's Lions Clubs, for the composer's grave at the Merion, Pennsylvania, cemetery: "James Bland put into ever-ringing verse and rhyme an expression of the feeling which all Virginians have for their state. *Carry Me Back to Old Virginny* tells in inspiring song the innate patriotism and love of native heath of all our people, white and Negro alike. Let us all hope that people of all races may continue to sing this song and mean the message it contains."

Though many people think that Bland's third notable composition, *Oh, Dem Golden Slippers!* is a genuine Negro spiritual, it was written in 1879 as a number to be sung by Sprague's Georgia Minstrels where, like *Dixie,* it was used as a walk-around. The Negro's imaginative picture of angels included wings, halos, and golden slippers:

Oh, dem golden slippers! Oh, dem golden slippers!
Golden slippers I'm gwine to wear
Because they look so neat;
Oh, dem golden slippers! Oh, dem golden slippers!
Golden slippers I'se gwine to wear
To walk de golden street.

James Bland merits a place in any discussion of our national songs, if only for the Virginia song which matches Stephen Collins Foster's *Old Folks at Home* as one of the finest songs with Negroes as their subjects.

The contribution of the Negro to our national music is unique. Their songs are American as well as Negro, and occupy a special and particular place in the life and musical heritage of our country.

☆☆☆☆☆☆☆☆☆☆

America
the Beautiful

America the Beautiful

O beautiful for spacious skies,
  For amber waves of grain,
For purple mountain majesties
  Above the fruited plain!
    America! America!
    God shed His grace on thee
And crown thy good with brotherhood
  From sea to shining sea!

O beautiful for pilgrim feet
  Whose stern, impassioned stress
A thoroughfare for freedom beat
  Across the wilderness!
    America! America!
    God mend thine every flaw,
Confirm thy soul in self-control,
  Thy liberty in law!

O beautiful for heroes proved
  In liberating strife,
Who more than self their country loved,
  And mercy more than life!
    America! America!

May God thy gold refine
Till all success be nobleness
 And every gain divine!

O beautiful for patriot dream
 That sees beyond the years
Thine alabaster cities gleam
 Undimmed by human tears!
  America! America!
  God shed His grace on thee
And crown thy good with brotherhood
 From sea to shining sea!

KATHARINE LEE BATES

1893; revised 1904.

CHAPTER 17

America the Beautiful

The martial words and music of most of our national patriotic songs stand in sharp contrast to the beauty of thought and the poetic sentiment of *America the Beautiful*. Many will agree that it tugs at the heart more than any other song which America has accepted as a proud possession.

America the Beautiful was not written under the stress of perilous times. Its purpose was solely to put into words the love for the varied natural beauties of the land and the ideal of brotherhood held by its citizens "from sea to shining sea."

Katharine Lee Bates, the poem's author, was a native New Englander directly descended from British and Irish ancestors who came to this country only fifteen years after the arrival of the *Mayflower*. Her father was the Congregational minister at Falmouth, Massachusetts, on the heel of Cape Cod, where she was born on August 12, 1859. Though he died a month after her birth, she passed her early years in this typically American village, attending its red-brick schoolhouse until the family—the widowed mother and her four children—moved to Grantville, now Wellesley Hills, when Katharine was twelve years old.

The young girl possessed an unusual heritage of culture and learning. Her mother had graduated from Mount Holyoke College in the days when few women attended an institution of higher learning. Her paternal grand-father had been president of Middlebury College, Vermont, for two decades in the early part of the nineteenth century. So it was entirely natural that she should enter Wellesley College in 1876. It was during her four years as a student there that she began writing poems. One of these poems, entitled *Sleep,* was accepted by William Dean Howells during her sophomore year for publication in the *Atlantic Monthly.*

Upon her graduation from Wellesley in 1880, at the age of twenty-one, she began the teaching career which was to cover forty-five years. Her first position was at the Natick, Massachusetts, high school, then at Dana Hall, a private school for girls. She was soon appointed as an instructor in English at her alma mater. Then began an association which, except for a few sabbatical years and several sum-mers of foreign study, continued until her retirement, with an honorary doctor's degree, in 1925, after forty years of continuous service with the institution.

During this time she composed scores of poems, the ma-jority of which were in praise of her country, its beauty and its ideals. In one long poem, *Land of Hope,* she catalogued some of the natural beauties she loved—the mountains, rock-based, cloudy-crested, and the prairies aripple with wheat. Two small volumes of her verse were published— one in 1887 and another in 1890—before she wrote *America the Beautiful*. Her collected poems, including all her best-known work, were printed in 1911.

Once, early in her teaching years, she was quarantined for smallpox for a month. This gave her time and leisure to write a story for young people, which she called *The Rose and the Thorn*. For this story she won a prize of seven hundred dollars, which paid for her first European trip. Her non-poetic output was continuous, including volumes of literary criticism, surveys of literature, editions of the classics, travel, and books for children. This varied literary work won her an honorary degree of Doctor of Literature from Middlebury College, her grandfather's college, in 1914, as well as a similar degree from Oberlin College.

Yet, had she never written a line except *America the Beautiful,* that poem alone would have brought her fame.

After a year of study abroad at Oxford, she returned to her teaching at Wellesley for the school year 1892–1893. She was invited to lecture at Colorado College, in Colorado Springs, along with Hamlin Garland and Woodrow Wilson, during the summer session of that year. On her cross-country trip she saw for the first time the wondrous glories of her native land, and she stopped for a day in Chicago, at the World's Columbian Exposition, where the exhibits impressed her anew with the seemingly unlimited resources and possibilities of the United States.

After the session at Colorado College had closed, a group of the Easterners on the faculty made an expedition to the top of nearby Pike's Peak. The ascent was made, as she later described it, "by the only method then available for people who were not vigorous enough to achieve the climb on foot nor sufficiently adventurous for burro-riding. Prairie wagons, their tailboards emblazoned with the traditional slogan 'Pike's Peak or Bust,' were pulled by horses up to the half-way house, where the horses were relieved by mules. We were hoping for half an hour on the summit but two of our party became so faint, in the rarefied air, that we were bundled into wagons again and started on our downward plunge so speedily that our sojourn on the peak remains in memory hardly more than one ecstatic gaze.

"It was then and there," she continued, "as I was looking out over the sea-like expanse of fertile country spreading away so far under those ample skies, that the opening lines of the hymn floated into my mind. When we left Colorado Springs the four stanzas were pencilled in my notebook, together with other memoranda, in verse and prose, of the trip."

The single experience of being surrounded by "purple mountain majesties," with the "spacious skies" overhead and the "fruited plain" at her feet, had so moved her that she was inspired to put down the words which she said came to her "almost like a vision, a trance." The verses lay buried in her notebook for two years thereafter, before she sent them to a church magazine, the *Congregationalist,* where they appropriately appeared in the issue of the Fourth of July, 1895.

The poem attracted a great deal of attention. Many tunes were written for it, so much so that Miss Bates rewrote it, striving to make the appeal as simple and direct as possible for its next appearance, in its present form, in the Boston *Transcript* of November 19, 1904. An accompanying article characterized it as "a thoroughly American production well-nigh perfect in poetry and in the most exalted strain as politics." At that time Thomas Bailey Aldrich first suggested that it ought to become the American national anthem.

Within twenty years it had been set to music almost a hundred times, and included in church hymnals and Sunday-school songbooks. World War I served to resurrect its popularity, and it was sung by soldiers, sailors, Boy Scouts, Girl Scouts, American Red Cross, Young Men's Christian Association, Young Women's Christian Association, the Society of Christian Endeavor, and scores of patriotic organizations. The noble words struck a responsive chord in the hearts and minds of the anxious people, and *America the Beautiful* became the poem most often printed during the war years.

Though associated with scores of different tunes, the most popular setting is Samuel Augustus Ward's hymn tune Materna (Latin for "motherly"), originally composed for *O Mother Dear, Jerusalem* in 1882. A lifelong resident of Newark, New Jersey, where he was a music dealer, Ward was for fourteen years the director of the local Orpheus Club.

In 1922 the composition was selected by the General Federation of Women's Clubs as its official song. It had long been incorporated into the hymnbooks of every Protestant denomination.

The National Federation of Music Clubs in 1926 instituted a contest to select a musical setting for the poem. But none of the nine hundred compositions submitted seemed to fill the need, so no award was made. Ward's Materna tune remained the most acceptable musical setting for this beautiful poem; today it is seldom, if ever, sung to any other melody. Concurrently the National Hymn Society pressed for its adoption as the country's national anthem. Though *The Star-Spangled Banner* was eventually chosen in 1931, *America the Beautiful* was a very close runner-up.

America the Beautiful is unique among national songs in that it is a true hymn rather than a mere patriotic song. H. Augustine Smith, the most prominent authority on music in religion, asserted that it has a rightful place in a hymnal "because it recognizes so clearly and emphasizes so fully the fact that America alone and unaided cannot make its dream come true. It is only God who can 'shed His grace' and 'crown good with brotherhood.' So the hymn is a prayer, a confession and a declaration of confidence in God's guidance." Another commentator has said, "Miss Bates' prayers, 'God mend thine every flaw,' 'May God thy gold refine,' and the repetition emphasizing 'God shed His grace on thee,' more than justify its inclusion in any book of sacred song." The words can be directly traced in its author's background and her 1893 Western trip. On this, her first journey across America, she had seen the "alabaster cities" of the last verse on her visit to the Chicago Exposition, with its gleaming white buildings, then called White City. This made a strong appeal to her patriotic feelings and, as she later wrote, "It was with this quickened and deepened sense of America that I went on, my New England eyes delighting in the wind-waved gold of the vast wheatfields."

Looking at the thrilling panorama of mountains and valleys as seen from the top of Pike's Peak, she was impressed by the "spacious skies" and the "purple mountain majesties." As a native of New England, she realized the great past of America, and the contributions of the Pilgrims whose "stern, impassioned stress" made "a thoroughfare for freedom across the wilderness." She hoped that the "alabaster cities" of the future would be "undimmed by human tears."

The expression of the brotherhood theme in the last verse appeared to account for the poem's popularity, for, she said, "Americans are at heart idealists, with a fundamental faith in human brotherhood." In 1928, when Miss Bates attended the annual meeting of the National Education Association in Minneapolis, the song was sung by a chorus of girls representing twenty different nationalities.

At that time she spoke of the many suggestions that had been made that she add a stanza to express international brotherhood as well. "It has not seemed easy to do that," she said, "for although I long for world brotherhood and am among those who look forward eagerly to the day when the United States shall enter the League of Nations, yet the song is long enough already, and is written for one special thing. So the best suggestion I can make is that when you sing the first stanza, you think of 'from sea to shining sea' as applying from the Pacific to the Atlantic, around the other way, and all the states in between, and that will include all the nations and all the people from sea to shining sea."

After Miss Bates' death on March 29, 1929, her old friend and fellow townsman, the historian Gamaliel Bradford, paid a tribute to the poem in an editorial in the Boston *Herald:* "There is in the poem the deepest, richest sense of the splendor of the material possession that has been given to us, and the impress upon every American citizen, every man, woman and child, to be worthy of that possession, to sustain it, to consecrate it, to ennoble it by developing the great qualities that can alone make any nation beautiful in the eyes of those who understand what spiritual beauty is."

Dorothy Burgess, a recent biographer of Miss Bates, aptly summarizes the qualities that make *America the Beautiful* an outstanding American national song in these words: "It is often said of the poem that it expresses for the millions of Americans their loftiest ideal of patriotism. For them, it rejoices in the gifts of their great country, it honors their dead, it pays homage to their past, it utters their aspirations, and it lifts their prayers. It is truly an American anthem."

☆☆☆☆☆☆☆☆☆

Songs of the
Spanish-American
War

CHAPTER 18

Songs of the
Spanish-American War

The Civil War proved to be the last in which the United States was involved to bring forth music of quality or permanence. Students of American musical history note that the popular songs of the next three wars—the War of 1898, and World Wars I and II—were undistinguished. Some say that the lack of good tunes was due to the fact that these wars were fought on foreign soil and to aid other countries. Men fighting "foreign" wars are comparatively undedicated and inclined to sing only those tunes which give them personal pleasure and make the grim business of war, for which Americans are constitutionally unfitted, a little more bearable.

The Spanish-American War of 1898 was the first in which the United States went to the defense of another country. The forces involved were comparatively few (a little over a quarter of a million men), the casualties proportionately small. From this war, however, our country emerged as a naval power. But the names highlighting the short conflict—the *Maine,* Admiral Dewey, Manila Bay, Santiago Bay, Guantanamo, Theodore Roosevelt and the Rough Riders, and San Juan Hill—failed to appeal to song-writers.

The musical legacy of this war is therefore limited to a few songs which reflect the taste of the period of the "gay Nineties," with its ragtime, minstrelsy, barbershop harmonies, and tear-jerking ballads.

The hits of the day were three in number, two sad and melancholy tunes, *On the Banks of the Wabash* and *Break the News to Mother,* and one rousing gay tune, *A Hot Time in the Old Town Tonight.* They may be examined today as museum pieces, and it is difficult to think of them as the favorites of fighting men, which is exactly what they were.

Paul Dresser's *On the Banks of the Wabash* seemed to have an appeal to every homesick soldier. Born in Terre Haute, Indiana, in 1857, Paul ran away to escape from his very religious family who were determined that he should become a priest. He was a medicine-wagon minstrel when he was sixteen. Then he became a well-known music hall singer and composer, his total of 260 songs being a record even among modern composers. He had no formal musical training, but seemed to be in tune with the times and to possess a feeling for what the public would want and accept.

The composer's real name was Dreiser, but because of the strenuous family objections to his career, he changed it to Dresser. Though the copyright date of *On the Banks of the Wabash* was 1899, it was in print during the Spanish-American War, and, according to his brother, the famous novelist Theodore Dreiser, fourteen years his junior, was conceived on a summer day in 1896.

In an introduction to a collection of his brother's compositions, Theodore Dreiser, by then famous in his own right, described how the song came into being. One day when they were together in the offices of Dresser's publishing company, Paul, thrumming at the piano, suddenly asked his brother, "Teddy, what do you suppose would make a good song these days? Why don't you give me an idea once in a while?"

Theodore retorted, "Why don't you write something about a state or a river? Look at *My Old Kentucky Home* and *Dixie*. Why don't you do something like that? For example, take Indiana, what's the matter with it—the Wabash River? It's as good as any other river and you were raised beside it."

"That's not a bad idea," Paul agreed "Why don't you write the words and let me put the music to them? We'll do it together."

"But I can't. I don't know how to do these things. You write it, and maybe I'll help."

After a little urging, Theodore took a piece of paper and scribbled a draft first verse and chorus, which was retained almost without change in the finished song. Paul read it, insisted it was excellent and suggested that his brother should write a second verse with a story in it, perhaps a girl. But his brother rejected the idea.

In the published version of *On the Banks of the Wabash*, Paul Dresser added the sweetheart he considered essential, and the song became the remembrance of a loved one who had strolled in the moonlight with the author, but had rejected his declared love and died:

Oh, the moonlight's fair tonight along the Wabash,
From the field there comes the breath of new-mown hay.
Thro' the sycamores the candle lights are gleaming,
On the banks of the Wabash, far away.

Within three months after its publication, the song was everywhere—in the papers, on the stage, on the street-organs, played by orchestras and bands, and sung the country over. Indiana belatedly adopted it as the state song on March 4, 1913, long after it had been a favorite song of the 1898 soldiers, and seven years after the composer's death.

Before the Spanish-American War began, Charles K. Harris had become recognized as the composer of the most popular tune of the early 1890's, *After the Ball,* which was fabulously successful and earned for him the reputation as the leading balladist of the time. He turned out scores of songs which were calculated to reduce the listener to tears. Many of the current plays were also designed to break the hearts of their audiences, for sticky sentimentality was then much in vogue.

One evening in 1897 Harris attended a performance of *Secret Service,* a play by and starring William Gillette, who is known for having created the character of Sherlock Holmes on the stage. This melodrama concerned a fifteen-year-old Southern boy who, in defiance of his parents, ran away to join the Confederate Army as a drummer boy. Wounded in battle, a corporal carried him off the field and took him to his plantation home. To the Negro butler who met them at the door, the lad said, "Break the news to mother."

Always on the alert for a song topic, Charles K. Harris wrote the phrase on his cuff in the darkened theater. The next day he wrote the first verse and chorus, and after lunch went to his barber's. He tells the rest of the story in his autobiography.

"Try as I might I could not think of a second verse or climax for the song. How to end the song with a punch puzzled me.

"While still in the barber's chair a thought came to my mind in a flash, and I cried out, 'I have it! I'm going to kill him!'

"The barber, who was shaving me at the time, became very much startled when he heard this remark and thought I had lost my reason.

" 'Joe, I tell you, he's got to die!' I shouted again.

"By this time the barber was convinced that there was something wrong with me. I was in a hurry to leave, and in less than two minutes was out of the chair, much to the re-lief of the barber. I had the last verse."

The song varied from the play; the young lad was with the Union Army, and as he lay wounded, he spoke to one of the fellow soldiers gathered around him (the chorus):

Just break the news to mother,
She knows how dear I love her,
And tell her not to wait for me,
For I'm not coming home;
Just say there is no other

Can take the place of mother,
Then kiss her dear sweet lips for me
And break the news to her.

In the second verse, a general standing by heard the words and, pushing through the crowd, recognized the lad as his son whom he had thought safely at home. "Forgive me, father, for I ran away" is the boy's dying phrase.

When Harris sang the song to his brother the response was a loud guffaw. "Charlie," he said, "there has been no war since 1865, and its memories are fast fading away. Another war is a long way off, so why in heaven's name have you written a soldier song?"

This reaction was so discouraging that Harris laid the composition aside. One day when his friend Paul Dresser was visiting him in Milwaukee, Harris sang *Break the News to Mother* to him. Dresser liked it, saying, "Charles, you have a big hit there, as big as *Wabash*." Harris had recommended the Indiana composer's song to the publisher who had accepted it, and by then it had sold over a million copies. So now Dresser was able to return his friend's favor by recommending it to *his* publisher. When issued in 1897, it attained little success at first, but the coming of the Spanish-American War gave it poignant meaning and it became a favorite of the soldiers.

But these two melancholy compositions yielded first place in popularity to *A Hot Time in the Old Town Tonight*. Its principal distinction was that it was completely gay and carefree, and therein lay the secret of its unprecedented success.

So popular was this song among the soldiers that the

Spaniards in Cuba were quite convinced that it was the American national anthem. The account of the victory of Colonel Theodore Roosevelt's Rough Riders at San Juan Hill on July 1, 1898, in a Paris newspaper described how the American soldiers gathered around their campfires and sang the American national anthem, *"Il Fera Chaud dans la Vielle Ville Ce Soir"* (There will be warm weather in the old city this evening)! Several years later, though admitting that the song had been often sung in camp and was the official song of his Rough Riders, President Roosevelt objected to the tune as a ragtime ballad unworthy of its popularity.

The original words and music were composed in 1886 by Theodore Metz, at that time the orchestra leader of McIntyre and Heath's Southern Minstrels. The troupe was passing through the village of Old Town, Louisiana, when they saw some Negro children putting out a fire near the railroad tracks. As a play on words, one of the minstrels remarked, "There'll be a hot time in the Old Town tonight," and Metz immediately used it as the title of a march.

Having meanwhile struck it rich in western mining, Metz returned to New York and set up a music publishing house. In 1896 he asked his friend Joe Hayden to compose Negro dialect words for his tune, using the same title, and the result was the minstrel song *A Hot Time in the Old Town Tonight:*

Come along get you ready, wear your bran, bran new gown
    For dere's gwine to be a meeting in that good, good old
        town,

Where you knowed ev'ry body and dey all knowed you
  And you've got a rabbit's foot to keep away de hoodoo,
When you hear that the preaching does begin,
  Bend down low for to drive away your sin
And when you gets religion you want to shout and sing
  There'll be a hot time in the old town tonight, my baby.

CHORUS

When you hear dem a bells go ding, ling, ling,
  All join 'round, and sweetly you must sing,
And when the verse am through, in the chorus all join in,
  There'll be a hot time in the old town tonight.

This was the song which was known by every soldier in the
Spanish-American War!

The year 1898 marked the height of minstrelsy, when the
Negro was caricatured in comic, or "coon," songs, and when
the Negro buck and wing, or clog, dance formed a major
part of such entertainment. *A Hot Time in the Old Town
Tonight* fitted this pattern admirably, even as *On the Banks
of the Wabash* and *Break the News to Mother* reflected the
taste for the sob ballads, or tear-jerkers.

☆☆☆☆☆☆☆☆☆☆

Songs of World War I

CHAPTER 19

Songs of World War I

The European War of 1914–1918 was the first truly world-wide war. The United States was late in becoming a partici-pant, abandoning its neutrality only when the struggle ap-peared to be overwhelming and our vast resources in men, money, and materials seemed necessary for victory over the Germans.

This was America's first full-scale "foreign" war. The United States Army, largely raised by the draft, totaled over four million, with a casualty record of 8 per cent. Almost every American citizen was affected in some way.

Our soldiers made the long trip overseas in an unprece-dented migration. The methods of fighting resulted in ap-palling casualties. The dugouts and trenches were primi-tive, and the mud and rain were never-ending. The life of the soldier had little glamour or comfort.

The soldiers of the other allied countries had been fight-ing for three years before our aid arrived. These soldiers—

English and British Empire, French, Italian, and Russian—
had already chosen their favorite songs, and the Americans
took up some of them, particularly those of the British,
whose language link served to make them appealing to
American ears.

As in the Spanish-American War, the light-hearted song
was triumphant among the soldiers. Europeans were puzzled because our boys in khaki seemed to treat the war almost as a picnic. Since most of them were draftees, the
appeal to "save the world for democracy" fell on deaf ears.
The American soldier risking his life merely wanted to
finish his task as quickly as possible, and was only too glad
to forget the grim reality of war whenever he could. American soldiers always seemed to be singing and whistling.
Their carefree spirit puzzled their fellow allies, who had
borne such a tremendous burden.

But hidden under the veneer of gaiety was a sincerity
and warmth of feeling in the heart of the American soldier.
He was not as carefree as he would have it appear.

The civilians on the home front were worried and lone-
some. A service flag was proudly displayed in the window of
practically very home, its blue star standing for a son, husband, or father in the armed forces. Keeping up morale was
a constant problem. The enforced separations created heavy
hearts. But they were proud of their soldier boys. Some of
the popular songs were directed to them rather than to the
men in uniform. The civilians felt closer to their absent
loved ones when they sang the same songs, hence many of
the songs of the soldiers became the songs of the people.

Three of the favorite soldier songs—*It's a Long Way to*

Tipperary, Pack Up Your Troubles, and *Keep the Home Fires Burning*—were already popular among the British and were readily accepted before American tunesmiths could get to work after the United States' entry in the war in 1917.

The first of these songs was *It's a Long Way to Tipperary.* Popularly known as *Tipperary,* it had been written in 1912 as a music hall (vaudeville) tune with no thought of using it as a war song. But the British soldiers liked its merry rhythm. The name of the author-composer has never been definitely established. Harry Williams' name is always mentioned, and if he was the author, the song which the Tommies preferred above all others was composed by an American!

It was said to have been written at Douglas Manor, Long Island, for a vaudeville skit. The song was rejected by several publishers, and Williams, who usually spent half of each year in London theaters, probably took it with him on a trip there in 1912, for it was shortly thereafter accepted by an English publishing firm.

Other accounts state that *Tipperary* was written in 1911 by Jack Judge, an Irish singer popular in London music halls, who admitted he was assisted by Williams. At first the song aroused little enthusiasm, but with the coming of the war it was taken over by the British soldiers. The words have nothing to do with the war; they merely reflect the jollity of an Irishman in London who longs for his beloved Tipperary and the sweetest girl he knows.

But this mattered not at all to the millions of soldiers who sang:

It's a long way to Tipperary,
  It's a long way to go.
It's a long way to Tipperary,
  To the sweetest girl I know.
Goodbye, Piccadilly,
  Farewell, Leicester Square,
It's a long way to Tipperary,
  But my heart's right there.

Some commentators have credited the appeal of the song to the yearning it expresses to be at home, that home not necessarily being in Ireland. A New York newspaper gave a capsule evaluation of the song: "A free and swinging lilt, a touch of humor, of sentiment, a dash of rough-and-ready patriotism." Few songs are more singable and simple, which may serve to explain *Tipperary*'s popularity. The British took it with them all over Europe, and it was their best marching song. The total sale of sheet-music copies was the phenomenal number of six million, one of the all-time highs in music publishing.

The second of the British songs taken over by the Americans was *Pack Up Your Troubles,* by George Asaf and Felix Powell. The English soldiers had begun singing it in 1915, when it was a number in a current London show, *Her Soldier Boy:*

Pack up your troubles in your old kit bag
  And smile, smile, smile;
While you've a lucifer to light your fag,
  Smile, boys, that's the style.

What's the use of worrying?
    It never was worth while,—SO—
Pack up your troubles in your old kit bag
    And smile, smile, smile.

The song lent itself to a rousing performance; it could
be literally shouted, and the final "SO—" could be an overwhelming burst of sound. The fact that two of the key
words ("lucifer" for match and "fag" for cigarette) were
English colloquialisms bothered American soldiers and
civilians not at all. Undoubtedly moved by its gaiety and
the urge to smile, smile, smile, they accepted the song without reservations.

The only rival of these light British songs was a masterpiece of its type, the haunting *Keep the Home Fires Burning,* the third song which the Americans took from the
British. The composer, Ivor Novello, possessed a superior
musical background and training which is reflected in the
musical quality of the song. He confessed that he wrote
it in the early days of the war excitement in England because his mother, an excellent musician, had one day urged
him to write something "to take the place of this bleak
Tipperary tune which has become so tiresome." Before he
had set himself to the task, she had written a song which he
considered so mediocre that he said to himself, "I *will*
show her."

The tune came to him as a veritable flash of inspiration
and was completed in ten minutes. He wanted to get away
from the life of the soldier and he wanted no humor. Families everywhere were being suddenly separated and were

filled with anxiety as the military might of the Germans began asserting itself. The idea of the home fires came to him suddenly and, in thinking of possible words he hit upon the phrase which became the title.

Having completed the melody, he telephoned a friend of his mother, Mrs. Lena Guilbert Ford, an American-born poet who had spent all her life in London, and sang the tune for her over the phone. He told her of his basic idea and theme, and she said, "I'll call you back." Within two hours, in a series of calls, they had completed the song exactly as it was later published. The result was a happy combination of melody and sentiment possessing, in its plea for courage in the absence of their loved ones, tremendous appeal to all civilians.

Strange as it seems, several publishers rejected *Keep the Home Fires Burning* until a comparatively minor firm accepted it late in 1915. There was never any question of the song's acceptance by the public, and it attained unheard of popularity, reaping huge financial returns in royalties for Novello (over 15,000 pounds in its first two years at a time when the pound was worth nearly five dollars). When the song reached the United States, which it did almost immediately, it became a powerful propaganda weapon. A recording made by the tenor John McCormack paid him almost $100,000 in royalties during the war.

Ivor Novello was the first composer to write a war song which was neither light-hearted nor vociferously patriotic. Besides having a tremendous appeal to Americans, *Keep the Home Fires Burning* deserves a place among our national ballads because the author of the words, Mrs. Ford, though an expatriate, was born in Elmira, New York. Mrs. Ford herself was not destined to keep the home fires burning until the end of the war. She was killed in an air raid on London in 1918.

But her words and the matchless melody of the twenty-one-year-old Englishman, Ivor Novello, have lived and will live in millions of hearts:

> They were summoned from the hillside,
>   They were called in from the glen,
> And the country found them ready
>   At the stirring call for men.
> Let no tears add to their hardships
>   As the soldiers pass along,
> And although your heart is breaking,
>   Make it sing this cheery song.
>
> CHORUS
> Keep the home fires burning
>   While your hearts are yearning,
> Though your lads are far away
>   They dream of home.
> There's a silver lining
>   Through the dark cloud shining,
> Turn the dark cloud inside out
>   Till the boys come home.

But there were other songs, composed by Americans for Americans, which attained as much popularity as the three already described.

Before entering the war, Americans had been hesitant

and divided. But once the step was taken, there was no holding back. And the greatest American song of the first World War, *Over There,* was written by George M. Cohan at the exact moment to strike fire. The sentiment "We'll all be over, we're coming over, and we won't be come back till it's over, over there" was perfectly timed.

Cohan was at the height of his fame when war for the United States became a reality. Born on the Fourth of July, 1878, he was a citizen proud of his country. Many of the most successful numbers in his musical plays were patriotic in tone; still well known are *Yankee Doodle Boy* (from *Little Johnny Jones,* 1904) and *You're a Grand Old Flag* (1905).

Starting his stage career when he was fifteen in a family song-and-dance act, the Four Cohans, he became successful in varied fields—as song-writer, actor, playwright, director, and manager. His musical comedies were unique in that they were truly American not only in their complete happiness and abandon, but in the patriotic choruses or finales that glorified the flag or appealed to patriotism. This dedication to an idea began when as a young boy George overheard a famous dancer say that it was time some one introduced the American flag on the stage.

When our country declared war on Germany on April 6, 1917, Cohan, like all others, was deeply affected. Before he went to his office the next morning he had looked again and again at the headlines in the paper. Seizing a piece of paper, he began writing the chorus of *Over There,* and completed it in half an hour. The verse, written while en route to New York City from his home on Long Island, was completed on his arrival; it was borrowed from an 1886 song *Johnny, Get Your Gun*. He first tried out the song while entertaining troops at Fort Myers, near Washington, but with little response from the weary soldiers in training there.

But when it was published, *Over There* was almost immediately popular. Presented at a Red Cross benefit, it quickly became a song of and for the people, sung by civilians at Liberty Loan rallies and benefits, and by soldiers in every situation:

> Over there, over there,
> Send the word, send the word, over there,
> That the Yanks are coming, the Yanks are coming,
> The drums rum-tumming everywhere. . . .

Over There by George M. Cohan; © copyright 1917/copyright renewal 1945 Leo Feist, Inc., New York, N.Y.; used by permission.

The inner rhymes of *Over There* are unusual and the music perfect for marching to the accompaniment of bands. The song occupies a special niche among patriotic tunes and is an outstanding example of a simple song with a tremendous human appeal. Its popularity in World War II was almost equally as great, proof of its enduring qualities.

During the rest of his career, until his death in November, 1942, Cohan turned away from composing, but he left a legacy of over five hundred songs and about forty plays. In his later years he gained fame as an actor. By act of Congress, dated June 29, 1936, he was presented with a gold medal "in belated recognition of his authorship of *Over There* and *Grand Old Flag*."

In contrast to the martial *Over There* was the sentimental ballad, *There's a Long, Long Trail,* which was nearly as appealing musically as its English counterpart, *Keep the Home Fires Burning*. It was never intended as a war ballad, and no one was more astounded by its acceptance than the young composer, Zo Elliott.

During his student years at Yale College he and a classmate, Stoddard King, collaborated on the annual campus shows. When they were seniors in 1913, they were asked to write some songs for a banquet of their fraternity in Boston. The boys always liked to hear new comic songs, but this time the team decided a "heart throb" ballad was needed.

One night while cramming for an examination, Elliott began humming a tune which he wrote down. King easily and quickly composed the words. At its performance the fraternity brothers failed to appreciate the composition, and in vain the toastmaster called for quiet. But Elliott liked it enough so that he submitted it to several publishers throughout the summer, though with no success.

That fall he enrolled at Trinity College, Cambridge, England, and often played and sang for his fellow students. One of them mentioned a comparatively obscure London firm that was looking for new and promising songs. They liked *There's a Long, Long Trail,* but in order to have it published Elliott had to pay for the expenses of the initial printing, to be repaid in royalties later.

At the opening of the war he was caught traveling in

Germany and was barely able to make his escape through Switzerland. He forgot about the song until a sizable sum in accrued royalty payments from the first few months' sales reached him. The song was therefore published in the United States in mid-1914 and soon was a national hit. When our country entered the war, the popularity of Elliott's song skyrocketed, and the net sales reached the unbelievable sum of three million dollars, far beyond any other of our war songs, even *Over There*.

This was a perfect song of home and the girl left behind. In those times of loneliness and fighting, the words struck a note of hopefulness for an anticipated time of peace:

> There's a long, long trail awinding
> Into the land of my dreams,
> Where the nightingales are singing
> And the white moon beams;
> There's a long, long night of waiting
> Until my dreams all come true;
> Till the day when I'll be going down
> That long, long trail with you.

Smiles (words by J. Will Callahan, music by Lee S. Roberts) was another wartime best-seller. The idea came to Roberts in 1917, just as America was on the verge of going to war. He was attending a convention of music dealers in Chicago where he heard a speaker tell about the value of smiles in business. Turning to a woman at his side, Roberts remarked, "There are smiles that make us happy, and smiles that make us blue."

He rushed to the piano and turned out the melody rapidly, sending it to his friend with the suggested theme. Callahan matched words to it in about half an hour, and not a note or word of the original manuscript was changed. Rejected by several publishers, the team issued it privately, and it gradually began being played by dance bands with success. Early in 1918, when America had a true need for smiles, it was published:

> There are smiles that make us happy,
> There are smiles that make us blue,
> There are smiles that steal away the tear-drops
> As the sunbeams steal away the dew.
> There are smiles that have a tender meaning
> That the eyes of love alone may see.
> And the smiles that fill my life with sunshine
> Are the smiles that you give to me.

Within six months 1,800,000 copies had been sold and the song was heard everywhere—on the vaudeville stage, in dance halls, on phonograph records and on player-piano rolls. The total sale was eventually three million copies, and the team split royalties of fifty thousand dollars.

The American soldier, however, was high-spirited and boisterous. And, above all, he wanted to sing. The Army responded to this urge by organizing a program of group singing, led by professional musicians, at the many training camps and embarkation points. Bands were recruited to add zest to the program.

The pocket-sized official songbook issued by the Army

contained eighty-five titles and included almost all our national songs. There were hymns, love ballads, and martial songs. But above all there were many humorous songs and slangy verses set to well-known tunes. One of these songs was known by every soldier.

K-K-K-Katy, subtitled *The Stammering Song,* the work of Geoffrey O'Hara, was successful because it lent itself to group singing and again showed that soldiers wanted to enjoy themselves and forget about the war:

> K-K-K-Katy, beautiful Katy,
> You're the only g-g-g-girl that I adore . . .

K-K-K-Katy by Geoffrey O'Hara; © copyright 1918/copyright renewal 1946 Leo Feist, Inc., New York, N.Y.; used by permission.

Another rousing song, perhaps liked because its singing could release accumulated tensions, was the revived *Hail! Hail! The Gang's All Here!,* composed by Theodore F. Morse in 1904. The soldiers particularly liked to boom out the phrase "what the h—— do we care." For that reason the song did not appear in most collections; and when it did, the objectionable word was omitted and "deuce" substituted for "hell":

> Hail! hail! the gang's all here,
> What the h - - - do we care
> What the h - - - do we care,
> Hail! hail! we're full of cheer,
> What the h - - - do we care, Bill.

The melody was derived from a tune in Gilbert and Sullivan's *Pirates of Penzance.*

A young man named Irving Berlin, who had gained prominence as the composer of *Alexander's Ragtime Band*, was drafted like any other able-bodied man, and found himself a private at Camp Upton, New York. By the time the encampment had become a training station for troops on their way overseas, Berlin had become a sergeant. He was asked to write and produce a camp show using soldier talent. The result was *Yip, Yip, Yaphank*, "a musical mess cooked up by the boys of Camp Upton."

Every soldier in the entire army became familiar with one of its humorous songs, for *Oh! How I Hate to Get Up in the Morning* struck an all-too-familiar note:

Oh! how I hate to get up in the morning,
Oh! how I'd love to remain in bed;
For the hardest blow of all, is to hear the bugler call:
You've got to get up, you've got to get up, you've got to
    get up this morning! . . .*

Among the songs which Berlin wrote for the show was a number called *God Bless America* which he had intended to use as a final number. However, the song did not seem to fit the mood he wanted, so he put it away and it remained entirely forgotten for twenty years.

To the soldiers, World War I was a singing war. As they themselves said, "Music keeps us from getting blue. We all have a country, a home and a girl, and music talks about these things without making you say anything."

* Copyright 1918 by Irving Berlin, copyright renewed; reprinted by permission.

The civilians, too, felt the need for songs to rally their spirits and to give them hope for the future. Entertainment by radio was not yet available, and a family had to make its own leisure-time music. They did it mostly through the piano and phonograph.

The former, upright or grand, was an essential piece of furniture in every home where it could be afforded. Popular music writing reached its peak during these World War I years. Tin Pan Alley poured out tunes which could be played, sung, and danced to, and every piano in the land was put to work. This explains the astronomical figures for sales of sheet music which have almost never since been equaled. The player-piano was available for those who could not themselves play the piano, and rolls, now almost never seen, took the place of the parlor pianist.

The phonograph had just become a popular instrument, and records, poor in sound quality as they were, blared out any and all tunes.

The unique feature of World War I was the recognition, for the first time, that music could play an important part in the lives of both soldiers and civilians. Songs were seen to be valuable allies as morale builders while the people lived through this terrible modern conflict which was intended to be "the war to end all war."

☆☆☆☆☆☆☆☆☆☆

God Bless America

God Bless America

God bless America,
   Land that I love,
Stand beside her and guide her
   Thru the night with a light from above;
From the mountains, to the prairies,
   To the oceans white with foam,
God bless America,
   My home, sweet home.
God bless America,
   My home, sweet home.*

IRVING BERLIN

1938

CHAPTER 20

God Bless America

The tale of Irving Berlin is a true American success story. From obscure birth and poverty he became the best known and most successful present-day composer of popular songs. And because he enjoyed and appreciated the blessings of his adopted country and the great opportunities it offered, he has sought to pay the debt he owes by singing of America. He has done this in many of his compositions, but never so effectively as in *God Bless America*, without question the most effective and popular national song of contemporary date.

The composer who later became known as Irving Berlin was born Israel Baline in Tuman, Russia, in 1888, and came to the United States with his parents and seven brothers and sisters when he was four years old. The family had made their escape when Cossacks had commenced the persecution and killing of Jews in the area. They arrived during the period when the tide of immigration was pouring thousands of Europeans through Ellis Island into New York City. Like the Balines, most of these newcomers remained in the tenement slums of the city.

Hence Israel's boyhood was passed on the lower east side, where he sold papers on the streets. His father died four years after the family's arrival, and the young boy found it necessary to contribute to their support. He had ambition and a gift for music, so he became a street singer along the Bowery and finally played piano and sang in saloons.

The young teenager soon discovered and made use of his talents for versification, composing the words to a song, published with his name as "I. Berlin." Though he received a royalty of a mere thirty-seven cents, he was embarked on his career. He became a singing waiter and thus learned all about what people would listen to and like. He turned out scores of verses on the sentimental subjects then so popular.

But his first success came with the publication of *Alexander's Ragtime Band* when he was twenty-three. From that time on he specialized in writing songs in the new rhythm of ragtime, which had originated in New Orleans. Sentimental ballads and tear-jerkers were no longer popular. The young composer was a leader in the new craze. He had further success in writing the words and music of several songs used in a production of the one and only Florenz Ziegfeld, and numbers for the most famous ballroom dancers of the day, Irene and Vernon Castle.

Then came the European war and Berlin did his bit by writing the soldier show *Yip, Yip, Yaphank*. One of the songs he did not use in the production was titled *God Bless America,* for he felt that its patriotic theme was not appropriate to a musical play in which the cast were already in uniform. During the 1920s and 1930s Berlin was the king of Tin Pan Alley, writing ballads and songs by the dozens for stage and the newly developed sound motion pictures. Some of these formed the background music for the dance routines of the team of Ginger Rogers and Fred Astaire.

But the war clouds were again gathering in Europe. The German persecution of the Jews affected Mr. Berlin greatly, and the threat to European and world peace troubled him. Hitler had invaded Austria early in 1938, and the Munich Pact, intended to forestall further expansion by the Nazis, was signed while the composer was visiting London. He felt that this danger, if it engulfed Europe, would mean another war, this time more devastating than that of 1914–1918, and that the United States would inevitably be drawn into such a conflict.

At that time radio was at the peak of its popularity, for television was still in an experimental stage. The singer Kate Smith was the undisputed queen of the air waves, and as she was planning a patriotic program for Armistice Day, 1938, she asked Mr. Berlin, who had returned to the United States, if he had a song which could be used to express the feelings of Americans about their country.

Fresh from Europe, he appreciated more than ever the blessings of freedom which his adopted country represented, and felt that he should write a patriotic song expressing his love for it. But he was not satisfied with his attempts at composition. Finally, he remembered the

number he had written but never used in 1917, and
brought it out.

Kate Smith first sang *God Bless America* to millions in
the radio audience on the evening of November 10, 1938.
Before long it was played everywhere on phonograph
records, in homes from sheet music, and by orchestras and
bands. Feeling that the dignity of the tune should be
preserved, Mr. Berlin forbade its being played as a dance
tune. He gave the exclusive radio performance rights of
the number gratis to Miss Smith.

There have been many who have thought that *God
Bless America* is worthy of being our national anthem.
The song's main quality is utter simplicity. Any one can
sing it, for the range is only eight notes. The words are
easy to memorize and remember.

In this composition Irving Berlin has magnificently
combined the major qualities of a true national song—
love of and pride in country, loyalty to it, gratitude for
its many blessings, and a prayer for divine protection.

God Bless America was published in 1939 by Mr.
Berlin's company, and for each copy sold he received the
unheard-of royalty of eight cents. By 1940 the song had
become a phenomenal success, and royalties were pouring
in. In that year he established a special trust called The
God Bless America Fund, from the proceeds of sales of
sheet music, phonograph records, and payments for performances on stage, radio and, later, television. The money
was to be contributed to the Boy Scouts and Girl Scouts,
which he believed were the organizations "best calculated
to promote unity of mind and patriotism."

The first payment to these organizations was over

$43,000. Since then the annual income has been steady, and $294,000 has been paid out as of January 1, 1960. The Boy Scouts of America now receive the full proceeds. The current trustees of the Fund are A. L. Berman, a New York lawyer and Gene Tunney, the former world's champion heavyweight boxer. Mrs. Theodore Roosevelt, Jr., the wife of the general who was killed in the second World War, was the third trustee until her death in May, 1960.

God Bless America is always sung at the conventions of both political parties, and by most patriotic societies and organizations. The tune is played at baseball games, roller skating rinks, bingo games, the President's birthday balls; in fact on almost any and every public occasion where a patriotic air appears to be appropriate. Many Americans prefer the song to *The Star-Spangled Banner* because it is simpler and more easily sung, and expresses more than mere loyalty to the flag. Certainly this deeply moving and simple air may be said to be our unofficial national anthem.

Irving Berlin was again active during World War II, producing and playing in the soldier show, *This Is the Army,* in which he reproduced the scene from *Yip, Yip, Yaphank* where he sang *Oh! How I Hate to Get Up in the Morning.* The entertainment toured the country, was made into a moving picture, played in England (earning $350,000 for British war charities), and finally toured all the major overseas United States Army commands throughout the world.

This Is the Army earned more than ten million dollars for the Army Relief Fund. Mr. Berlin also wrote songs for the defense bond program of the Treasury Department,

Navy Relief, the American Red Cross, and the March of Dimes, donating the royalties to the causes each honored. For his contribution to the war effort, he was decorated with the Army's Medal of Merit.

To date Irving Berlin has written over a thousand songs, many of which are familiar today—*Alexander's Ragtime Band, Always, Remember, Blue Skies, A Pretty Girl Is Like a Melody, Easter Parade,* and *White Christmas.*

Innumerable honors have been heaped upon this truly outstanding American. He has received many citations and plaques from various organizations such as the National Conference of Christians and Jews, the National Committee of Music Appreciation, and the National Association for American Composers and Conductors. Scholarships have been established in his name.

But he has himself admitted that the award of which he is most proud was the gold medal authorized by the United States Congress, presented to him by the President on February 18, 1955. On one side is Mr. Berlin's profile, on the reverse the inscription "Presented to Irving Berlin by President Eisenhower in national recognition and appreciation of services in composing many popular songs, including *God Bless America.*"

When legislation authorizing the striking of this medal was passed, the New York *Times* editorially stated: "Irving Berlin has not only given the public music that it loved, he has also given his time and talents in two wars. . . . There couldn't be a more popular law than the one that now gives Mr. Berlin his medal. May he wear it for many years to come."

☆☆☆☆☆☆☆☆☆☆

Songs of World War II

CHAPTER 21

Songs of World War II

While the United States stood on the sidelines as Europe was being engulfed in full-scale war for the second time within the twentieth century, the people were singing *God Bless America* and hoping that the "storm clouds far across the sea," of which Irving Berlin spoke, might possibly, by some miracle, disperse so that our country need not again become involved in a foreign war.

Americans watched in mounting anxiety as the Nazi juggernaut advanced ever forward. United States composers wrote a number of songs sympathetic to the countries who were fighting for their very existence. England's struggle was recognized in *The White Cliffs of Dover* and *There'll Always Be an England*. Holland's fall was treated in *My Sister and I,* and the French capital's in *The Last Time I saw Paris.*

When Pearl Harbor was attacked on December 7, 1941, the United States was no longer an observer offering aid through lend-lease operations, but became a full-scale participant in the struggle which was to extend beyond the continent of Europe to every corner of the world. And in these faraway places American soldiers were to fight side by side with their allies in a truly international war of an extent never before even dreamed of. The "make the world safe for democracy" slogan of the first World War became even more true than in 1914–1918.

This struggle affected the life of every American far more than any war since our own Civil War. The development and perfection of weapons of destruction made the individual soldier a mere cog in a war machine of unprecedented strength and power. The statistics on numbers of participants, casualties, and cost stagger the imagination. And because of the major role played by the United States in its contributions of manpower, money, and supplies, one might reasonably expect that poets and songwriters would have been sufficiently inspired to produce stirring compositions of lasting merit, which would, through repetition and popular acceptance, become national songs.

But the plain and inexplicable truth is that no song of the many turned out proved to have any merit, much less any of the qualities making for permanence. The hope that a great war song would spring from the inspiration of a poet and composer was never realized. One of the contemporary radio music conductors expressed doubt that a great American song might come out of the war when, in 1943, he said: "Writing a war song is like making a Stradivarius violin. When the right man comes along at just the right time, he'll write *the* war song. Perhaps the circumstances won't bring the man and the mood together in this war."

He proved to be right. Not a single composition of any lasting value was written. On the contrary, the output of Tin Pan Alley was notably mediocre, even banal. The power of the radio, the record-player, and the jukebox (over 400,000 were in operation), which could have brought a great song into every home and heart was devoted to completely undistinguished music. With the exception of *God Bless America,* the world of music made no contribution to the war effort. Students of the period are still baffled by the fact that this greatest of all our country's wars was musically so impotent.

The blame for the lack of a good song, much less a great song, has been put on the publishing business which, controlling the musical output, may have made it impossible for a song of quality, if such was written, to reach the people. Sheet-music sales declined; a sale of 300,000 copies of a song marked it as a hit, compared with the figures of a million for many songs published during World War I. Phonograph records jumped in popularity. The radio, which was an ideal medium for spreading a song and making it popular through constant repetition, was powerless because no song was produced which was worthy of such widespread performance.

A list of the popular American songs of the period indicates the lack of great, even good, compositions. Certainly *Praise the Lord and Pass the Ammunition, Remember Pearl Harbor,* and *I Am an American* cannot be considered moving. Sentimental ballads such as *No Love, No*

Nuthin', Till My Baby Comes Home, Goodnight, Wherever You Are, and *I Lost My Heart at the Stage Door Canteen* were not of lasting value. The civilian non-war songs, like *The Hut-Sut Song, You Are My Sunshine, Deep in the Heart of Texas,* and *Mairzy-Doats,* were far removed from the grim realities of war.

Only one song from a professional composer, Irving Berlin's *White Christmas,* possessed an appeal to the heart. He wrote it for a Bing Crosby–Fred Astaire motion picture, *Holiday Inn,* in 1942. This was the time when the American war effort was gaining momentum, and our soldiers were in distant places in every corner of the world. Christmas day in 1942 was the first when the loneliness of the soldier in strange parts of the world and the civilians in their homes was accented. Mr. Berlin's simple song was thus able to touch every heart, and may be considered the sole popular song of World War II:

> I'm dreaming of a white Christmas,
> Just like the ones I used to know;
> Where the tree-tops glisten
> And children listen to hear sleigh bells in the
>   snow. . . .*

Music, however, played a great part in the lives of the soldiers. During the first World War the armed forces had learned the value of music to morale. This time the fighting man was provided with a well-rounded program through trained song leaders, band directors, and the distribution of Hit Kits, a series of brochures giving the words and music

---

* Copyright 1942 by Irving Berlin; reprinted by permission.

of the songs currently popular at home, V-Discs, vinyl non-breakable records of all types of compositions and an Army and Navy songbook.

While including the words of many of our recognized national songs, the major titles included were those of World War I, some cowboy and Western tunes, and the songs of the various services. The latter may be considered the true songs of the second World War. Even though most of them were written long before, they did not achieve prominence until the early 1940s. The men in uniform and the civilians were to accept and sing these tunes—*The Army Air Corps* (now *The U.S. Air Force*), *Anchors Aweigh, The Caissons Go Rolling Along* and *The Marines' Hymn*—until they became the true national songs to come out of the war.

The development of American air power was one of the phenomena of the last war. After the almost primitive flying machine of 1918, the newly developed sky-birds were ready to play a major role in this conflict. The Army Air Corps took its place as an integral part of the United States' military might. This branch of the service was almost new, and it had no official song. But the gathering clouds of war produced the needed tune, *The U.S. Air Force,* written in 1939 by Robert M. Crawford.

The forty-year-old author-composer, born in Alaska, had gained his musical experience while at Princeton University, where he directed the glee club, conducted the orchestra, and wrote several of the student musical productions during the early 1920s. After graduation he studied abroad and became a conductor, singer, and composer. When he wrote the song he was not yet an airman, but in 1942 he joined the Air Transport Command as a major. Since 1947 he has been on the music faculty of the University of Miami.

An acceptable service song must meet several requirements. It must express the spirit of the branch of the service it honors. It must be uncomplicated and singable, even to the tone-deaf or the monotone, who can hum or whistle rather than sing. And, finally, it must have a regular cadence so that it can be shouted lustily while the singers are in marching formation.

The U.S. Air Force meets all these conditions. Its lusty love of life and carefree defiance mark the spirit of our airmen:

> Off we go into the wild blue yonder,
>   Climbing high into the sun;
> Here they come, zooming to meet our thunder,
>   At 'em, boys, give 'er the gun!
> Down we dive, spouting our flame from under,
>   Off on one helluva course! *
> We live in fame or go down in flame—HEY!
> Nothing'll stop the U.S. Air Force. †

The complete song has three additional verses. *The U.S. Air Force* won a thousand-dollar prize offered by *Liberty* magazine early in the war, and was sung by all the other branches of the service and civilians as well, for it possessed an immediate and infectious appeal.

---

* *To avoid controversy from the squeamish, "terrible" was to be substituted for "helluva" in radio performances.*

† Copyright 1939, 1942, 1951 by Carl Fischer, Inc., New York.

The official Navy song, *Anchors Aweigh,* was written in 1906, but it did not find its way outside the United States Naval Academy at Annapolis, Maryland, until the last war. The words were the work of Midshipman Alfred H. Miles of the class of 1907, leader of the chapel choir. The music was composed by Lieutenant Charles A. Zimmermann, the Academy's bandmaster.

Dedicated to the class of 1907, *Anchors Aweigh* was designed for the annual Army-Navy football game, and was first sung in November, 1906, during the break at the half, when the Academy band marched on the field. As a rallying and "pep" song, it urged the Navy blue to victory over the Army gray.

For twenty years thereafter it was sung by midshipmen only at the annual football classic. But in 1926, with added verses by Midshipman Royal Lovell of that year's class, it was first published by the Academy's Trident Literary Society as *Anchors Aweigh,* as we know it today:

> Anchors aweigh, my boys,
>> Anchors aweigh;
> Farewell to college joys,
>> We sail at break of day, day, day, day—

The song's composer, Zimmermann, died in 1916 after thirty-four years as leader of the Academy band and chapel organist. Miles served throughout World War II, retiring in 1945 with the rank of commander. *Anchors Aweigh* has been called "a swinging, throbbing military march that puts rhythm in the feet and fire in the heart."

The third great service song, *The Caissons Go Rolling Along,* the official song of the artillery, was written by a West Point graduate of the class of 1904, Edmund L. Gruber, while serving in the Philippines as an Artillery Corps first lieutenant in 1908:

> Over hill, over dale,
>   We have hit the dusty trail,
> And those caissons go rolling along.
> "Counter march!" "Right about!"
>   Hear those wagon soldiers shout,
> While those caissons go rolling along.
>
> CHORUS
> For it's Hi! Hi! Hee! in the Field Artillery,
> Call off your numbers loud and strong;
> And where'er we go,
> You will always know
> That the caissons are rolling along.
>
> To the front, day and night
>   Where the doughboys dig and fight
> And the caissons go rolling along.
> Our barrage will be there
>   Fired on the rocket's flare
> While those caissons go rolling along.

The second verse, strangely enough, did not attain much acceptance until the early 1930s. It had, however, become known as a rousing band selection arranged in 1918 by the great John Philip Sousa, titled *The Field Artillery March,* first played at a Liberty Loan benefit concert at the New York Hippodrome. Gruber continued in his army career, finally attaining the rank of brigadier general. *The Caissons Go Rolling Along* is another excellent example of a stirring military march.

The fourth distinguished service song was *The Marines' Hymn,* printed in 1919, but not generally popular until the second World War. The music was adapted from Jacques Offenbach's operetta *Geneviève de Brabant,* first performed in Paris in 1859. The author of the words remains anonymous, but was undoubtedly a Marine officer who was a member of a battalion of forty men who were the first to enter Mexico City in 1847 during our Mexican War.

This explains the phrase "From the Halls of Montezuma." "The shores of Tripoli," of course, refers to the participation of the Marine Corps in the war against the Barbary pirates in 1805. The Marines have had a proud record in all our wars, generally offering assistance as a standby reserve force to back up the Army and the Navy in strategic campaigns. Several times in our country's history, they have been sent to various parts of the world, such as China and Nicaragua, to quell local outbreaks.

The Marines' Hymn admirably expresses the pride of the organization:

> From the Halls of Montezuma
> To the shores of Tripoli;
> We fight our country's battles
> On the land as on the sea.

First to fight for right and freedom
And to keep our honor clean,
We are proud to claim the title
Of United States Marine.

Though the infantry is the largest group in our military
establishment, no song has yet been written worthy of acceptance as official. The infantryman has had to be content
to sing the songs of World War I and those of the other
services. The official song of the Coast Artillery, *Crash On!
Artillery,* copyrighted in 1935, is almost unknown, as is
Semper Paratus, the official song of the United States Coast
Guard, composed by Captain Francis S. Van Boskerck in
1928. The Merchant Marine's *Heave To, My Lads, Heave
Ho!,* written by Lieutenant Jack Lawrence in 1943, is also
little known. The women in the service during World War
II—the Army Nurse Corps and the Women's Army Corps
(WAC)—both had official songs of only temporary note.

The Korean War of 1950–1953, in which United States
forces participated with other members of the United Nations family, produced no music of any worth.

A musical development before and during the period
the second World War was the emergence of a truly Ame
can music composed for the stage. Some of the tunes f
musical productions, such as *Porgy and Bess, Oklahe
Show Boat,* and the like, with the passing of the yea
become accepted as national songs. Certainly, the
sitions of Kern, Romberg, Friml, and the team of
and Hammerstein, to name but a few, have ma
pression on the American people.

But the tunes which have endured and been accepted as part of our legacy as Americans can never be replaced. There may be future additions, but those that have lived from the past will never be supplanted in popular acceptance and favor.

They stand, and will continue to stand, as examples of the earnest prayer of Oliver Wendell Holmes:

> One flag—one land,
> One heart—one hand,
> One nation, Evermore.

☆☆☆☆☆☆☆☆☆

Reading List

READING LIST

GENERAL BOOKS

Banks, Louis A. *Immortal Songs of Camp and Field.* Burrows Bros. Co., 1899.

Brinton, Howard F. *Patriotic Songs of the American People.* Tuttle, Morehouse & Taylor Co., 1900.

Chase, Gilbert. *America's Music, from the Pilgrims to the Present.* McGraw-Hill, 1955.

Dolph, Edward A. *Sound Off!: Soldier Songs from the Revolution to World War II.* Farrar and Rinehart, 1942.

Ewen, David. *Panorama of American Popular Music.* Prentice-Hall, 1957.

Howard, John Tasker. *Our American Music: Three Hundred Years of It.* 3d ed. rev., Crowell, 1954.

Howard, John Tasker and George K. Bellows. *Short History of Music in America.* Crowell, 1957. (An abridgment of the above title.)

Kobbé, Gustav. *Famous American Songs.* Crowell, 1906.

Lyons, John H. *Stories of Our American Patriotic Songs.* Vanguard, 1942.

Montgomery, Elizabeth R. *The Story Behind Popular Songs.* Dodd, Mead, 1958.

Nettl, Paul. *National Anthems* . . . tr. by Alexander Gode. N.Y., Storm Publishers, 1952.

Smith, Nicholas. *Stories of Great National Songs.* 2d ed. The Young Churchman Co., 1899.

Sonneck, Oscar G. T. *Report on "The Star-Spangled Banner," "Hail, Columbia," "America," "Yankee Doodle."* Government Printing Office, 1909.

Spaeth, Sigmund. *History of Popular Music in America.* Random House, 1948.

Van Doren, Carl C. and Carl L. Carmer. *American Scriptures.* Boni and Gaer, 1946.

> References are made to these books by author in the reading lists for chapters below when the songs are extensively treated in these books.

CHAPTER 2: Yankee Doodle

Banks, 41–49.

Brinton, 9–14.

Howard, 113–18.

Kidson, Frank. "Some Guesses about 'Yankee Doodle,' " *Musical Quarterly,* Vol. 3 (January, 1917), 98–103.

Kobbé, 125–40.

Lyons, 17–22.

Nettl, 175–77.

Smith, 23–32.

"Song of the American Revolution," *Etude,* Vol. 55 (July, 1937), 427–28, 485.

Sonneck, 79–156.

CHAPTER 3: Hail, Columbia

Ashton, Leonora S., "President's March: Hail, Columbia," *Etude,* Vol. 71 (July, 1953), 54–55.

Banks, 67–74.

Brinton, 15–18.

Howard, 118–21.

Kobbé, 140–45.

Lyons, 23–28.

Nettl, 178–80.

Smith, 39–43.

Sonneck, 43–72.

CHAPTER 4: The Star-Spangled Banner

Banks, 53–63.

Brinton, 19–22.

Fisher, William A. "Origin of 'The Star-Spangled Banner,'" *Etude*, Vol. 59 (February, 1941), 89.

Griffith, Eloise R. *National Anthems and How They Came to Be Written*. Boston, Christopher House,1952, 11–15.

Howard, 121–26.

Kimball, Frank W. "Star Spangled Banner," *Etude*, Vol. 53 (July, 1935), 390, 434.

Kobbé, 101–22.

Lyons, 9–16.

McNeil, A. W. "Star Spangled Banner," *Etude*, Vol. 55 (July, 1937), 432, 480, 488.

Nettl, 170–80.

Phillips, Cabell. "O Say Can You Sing It?" *New York Times Magazine*, May 18, 1958, 16, 83–85.

Smith, 44–55.

Sonneck, 7–42.

Sonneck, Oscar G. T. *"The Star-Spangled Banner."* Government Printing Office, 1914.

U.S. National Park Service. *Fort McHenry National Monument and Historical Shrine*. Washington, Government Printing Office, 1942 (National Park Handbook 5).

Van Doren and Carmer, 286–92.

Weybright, Victor. *Spangled Banner: The Story of Francis Scott Key*. Farrar and Rinehart, 1935.

World Almanac, 1960, 642.

CHAPTER 5: Home, Sweet Home

Bullard, F. Lauriston. "The Story of 'Home, Sweet Home' and John Howard Payne," *Musician*, Vol. 18 (April, 1913), 227–29, 278.

Devlin, D. J. "He Wrote the Most Endearing Song," *Mentor,* Vol. 17 (February, 1929), 32–35.

Dunham, Franklin G. "The True Story of 'Home, Sweet Home,'" *Musician,* Vol. 28 (August, 1923), 13, 23.

Engel, Carl. *Discords Mingled.* Knopf, 1931, 35–48.

Kobbé, 3–31.

Overmyer, Grace. *America's First Hamlet.* New York University Press, 1957, 202–38.

Ridgway, Gertrude M. " 'Home, Sweet Home' One Hundred Years After," *Outlook,* Vol. 133 (May 16, 1923), 896–900.

Smith, 3–31.

Van Doren and Carmer, 298–301.

Woolf, Samuel J. "The Romance of Home, Sweet Home and its Author," *Etude,* Vol. 65 (September, October, 1947), 484, 494, 540; 564, 593.

CHAPTER 6: America

Brinton, 23–32.

Cooke, James F. "World's Most Widely Sung Tune: God Save the King," *Etude,* Vol. 73 (June, 1955), 16, 62–63.

Griffith, Eloise R. *National Anthems and How They Came to Be Written.* Boston, Christopher House, 1952, 24–29.

Howard, 126–28.

Kimball, Frank W. "America," *Etude,* Vol. 55 (July, 1937), 434.

Kobbé, 145–51.

Lyons, 29–34.

Maginty, Edward A. " 'America': the Origin of its Melody," *Musical Quarterly,* Vol. 20 (July, 1934), 259–66.

Nettl, 34–48.

Scholes, Percy A. *God Save the Queen! The History and Romance of the World's First National Anthem.* Oxford University Press, 1954, 190–200.

Smith, 56–71.

Sonneck, *Report,* 73–78.
"Who Wrote 'America'?" *Etude,* Vol. 57 (November, 1939), 700, 760.

CHAPTER 7: Columbia, the Gem of the Ocean
Banks, 77–83.
Brinton, 39–42.
Lyons, 35–38.
Smith, 72–76.

CHAPTER 8: Old Folks at Home
Banks, 227–34.
Butterfield, Roger. "The Legend of Stephen Foster," *Saturday Evening Post,* Vol. 226 (February 6, 1954), 30, 104–6.
Chase, 283–300.
Howard, 184–97.
Howard, John Tasker. *Stephen Foster, America's Troubadour.* Crowell, 1953.
Kobbé, 35–56.
McCleary, Anna L. "My Old Kentucky Home; an 85-year-old Folk Song and Something of its History," *Etude,* Vol. 57 (May, 1939), 299, 335.
Montgomery, 5–11.
Overmyer, Grace. *Famous American Composers.* Crowell, 1944, 35–54.

CHAPTERS 9–15: Civil War Songs
Harwell, Richard B. *Confederate Music.* University of North Carolina Press, 1950.
Heaps, Willard A. and Porter W. *The Singing Sixties.* University of Oklahoma Press, 1960.
Howard, 255–68.
Spaeth, 137–74.

White, William C. *A History of Military Music in America.* Exposition Press, 1944, 66–82.

Ziff, Larzer. "Songs of the Civil War," *Civil War History,* Vol. 2 (September, 1956), 7–28.

CHAPTER 9: Dixie

Banks, 109–22.

Barbee, David R. "Who Wrote Dixie?," *Musical Digest,* Vol. 3 (May, 1948), 6–9.

Brinton, 49–59.

Chase, 272–77.

Fredericks, Pierce G. "Dixie's Northern Anthem," *New York Times Magazine,* November 10, 1957, 28–29.

Harwell, Richard B., ed. *The Confederate Reader.* Longmans, Green, 1957, 24–29.

Howard, 255–58.

Kobbé, 59–78.

Lyons, 39–45.

Nathan, Hans. "Dixie," *Musical Quarterly,* Vol. 35 (January, 1949), 60–84.

Smith, 179–92.

Smith, W. H. "The Story of Dixie and its Picturesque Composer," *Etude,* Vol. 52 (September, 1934), 524.

Street, James H. "In Dixie Land," *Reader's Digest,* Vol. 31 (August, 1937), 45–46.

CHAPTER 10: Maryland, My Maryland

Brinton, 78–83.

"How 'Maryland, My Maryland' Was Written," *Bookman,* Vol. 43 (July, 1916), 481–85.

Kobbé, 166–69.

Library of Southern Literature. New Orleans, 1907. Vol. 10, pp. 4309–14; Vol. 16, 68–71.

Lyons, 47–52.

Randall, James Ryder. *Poems.* Ed. with introduction and notes

by Matthew Page Andrews. Tandy-Thomas Co., 1910, 1–34.
Smith, N., 193–200.
Uhler, John Earle. "James Ryder Randall in Louisiana," *Louisiana Historical Quarterly*, Vol. 21 (April, 1938), 532–46.

CHAPTER 11: The Battle-Cry of Freedom

Banks, 125–33, 171–80.
Brinton, 60–67.
Epstein, Dena J. " 'The Battle-Cry of Freedom,' " *Civil War History*, Vol. 4 (September, 1958), 307–18.
Lyons, 53–57.
Smith, N., 93–107, 127–35.
Ward, Lydia A. C. "George F. Root and His Songs," *New England Magazine*, new series, Vol. 13 (January, 1896), 555–70.

CHAPTER 12: John Brown's Body

Banks, 97–106.
Brinton, 43–48.
Kimball, George. "Origin of the John Brown Song," *New England Magazine*, new series, Vol. 1 (1890), 371–76.
Kobbé, 155–62.
Smith, N., 72–92.
Stutler, Boyd P. " 'John Brown's Body,' " *Civil War History*, Vol. 4 (September, 1958), 251–60.

CHAPTER 13: The Battle Hymn of the Republic

Bakeless, Katherine L. *Glory, Hallelujah! The Story of The Battle Hymn of the Republic*. Lippincott, 1944.
Banks, 159–67.
Brinton, 71–77.
Hostetter, Helen P. "Sing It Again! 'Glory, Glory, Hallelujah!': the Romance of a Great American Patriotic Hymn," *Etude*, Vol. 60 (May, 1942), 294, 338.
Lyons, 59–65.

Smith, N., 108–20.

Tharp, Louise Hall. "The Song That Wrote Itself," *American Heritage,* Vol. 8 (December, 1956), 10–13, 100–01.

Van Doren and Carmer, 293–97.

Woollcott, Alexander. "She Sounded Forth the Trumpet," *Reader's Digest,* Vol. 40 (May, 1942), 49–50.

CHAPTER 14: Marching Through Georgia

Banks, 137–45, 193–96.

Brinton, 103–5.

Kobbé, 163–65.

Lewis, Lloyd. *Sherman, Fighting Prophet.* Harcourt, Brace, 1932, 613–14, 619–20, 632–33.

"Our Hymn of Hate: Marching Through Georgia," *Literary Digest,* Vol. 55 (July 21, 1917), 27–28.

Smith, N., 136–48.

CHAPTER 15: Other Civil War Songs

Banks, 149–55, 181–92, 217–26.

Brinton, 84–100.

Smith, N., 121–26, 153–56.

CHAPTER 16: Songs of the Negro

Butcher, Margaret J. *The Negro in American Culture.* Knopf, 1956, 40–56.

Chase, 232–58.

Ewen, 53–63.

Howard, 623–32.

Locke, Alain. *The Negro and His Music.* Washington, Associates in Negro Folk Education, 1936.

Odum, Howard W., and Guy B. Johnson. *The Negro and His Songs.* University of North Carolina Press, 1925.

James A. Bland

Daly, John. *A Song in His Heart.* Winston, 1951.

Hughes, Langston. *Famous Negro Music Makers*. Dodd, Mead, 1955, 27–34.
Montgomery, 12–16.

CHAPTER 17: America the Beautiful
Burgess, Dorothy. *Dream and Deed: The Story of Katharine Lee Bates*. University of Oklahoma Press, 1952, 97–106.
Lyons, 67–72.
Smith, H. Augustine. *Lyric Religion*. Century, 1931, 272–75.

CHAPTER 18: The Spanish-American War
Spaeth, 275–82.
Sullivan, Mark. *Our Times*. Scribner's, 1937. Vol. I, *The Turn of the Century*, 243–67.

CHAPTER 19: Songs of World War I
Dolph, 79–184.
Spaeth, 341–43, 397–98, 403–4.
Van Dyke, Catherine. "Music in the War," *Harper's Weekly*, Vol. 61 (July 31, 1915), 105–6.

Keep the Home Fires Burning
Noble, Peter. *Ivor Novello*. London, Falcon Press, 1951, 53–78.

Over There
Montgomery, 63–70.
Paris, Leonard. *Men and Melodies*. Crowell, 1954, 36–48.

There's a Long, Long Trail
Elliott, Zo. " 'There's a Long, Long Trail A-winding'; Story of a Song That Earned Three Million Dollars," *Etude*, Vol. 58 (February, 1940), 79–80.

CHAPTER 20: God Bless America
"Badgered Ballad: 'God Bless America,' " *Time*, Vol. 36 (September 30, 1940), 60.

Ewen, David. *The Story of Irving Berlin*. Holt, 1950.
Frazier, George. "Irving Berlin: Melody Maker Supreme," *Reader's Digest*, Vol. 51 (December, 1947), 92–94.
Paris, Leonard. *Men and Melodies*. Crowell, 1954, 94–106.
"Ragtime to Riches," *Newsweek*, Vol. 31 (June 14, 1948), 84–85.

CHAPTER 21: Songs of World War II

Desmond, John. "Tin Pan Alley Seeks the Song," *New York Times Magazine*, June 6, 1943, 14.
Howard and Bellows, 325–27.
Lederman, Minna. "Songs for Soldiers," *American Mercury*, Vol. 57 (September, 1943), 296–301.
Williamson, Samuel T. "Singing Army?" *New York Times Magazine*, November 15, 1942, 12–13.

White Christmas
Montgomery, 141–46.

☆☆☆☆☆☆☆☆☆

Index

INDEX

NOTE: *See also Title Index following this index.*

☆☆☆☆☆☆☆☆☆

Title Index

NOTE: *Song titles are not italicized in this index.*